NA 737
.W7
J3

Jacobs, Herbert Austin.
     Frank Lloyd Wright; America's greatest
architect [by] Herbert Jacobs. New York,
Harcourt, Brace & World [1965]

     223 p. illus., ports. 21 cm.

     Bibliographical references included in "Notes"
(p. [214]-217)

     1. Wright, Frank Lloyd, 1869-1959. I. Title.

     NA737.W7J3   921   65-25306
                           W949j

□ Frank Lloyd Wright

DISCARD

☐ Herbert Jacobs

Frank Lloyd Wright
America's Greatest Architect

☐

☐

☐

☐ Illustrated with photographs

Harcourt, Brace & World, Inc., New York

The "footnote" numbers in the text refer to printed and other sources of quoted material, which are listed by chapter in the *Notes* section at the back of the book.

The author and the publisher acknowledge with thanks the permission from Duell, Sloan & Pearce to quote passages from *An Autobiograhy* by Frank Lloyd Wright, copyright, 1943, by Frank Lloyd Wright; and from G. P. Putnam's Sons to quote from *My Father Who Is on Earth* by John Lloyd Wright, copyright, 1946, by John Lloyd Wright.

☐ Foreword

Much of the material in this book is based on twenty-five years of fairly frequent contact with Frank Lloyd Wright as client, friend, and reporter. He designed three houses for me, two of which were built, and the reader will rightly guess that I am the "journalist" who commissioned the moderate-cost house described in Chapter 11. Over the years, first for the *Milwaukee Journal,* and later for the *Capital Times,* of Madison, Wisconsin, I was extensively engaged in writing and photography dealing with Mr. Wright's activities.

I am grateful to Edgar Tafel, New York architect, long-time friend and for many years an apprentice under Frank Lloyd Wright, for valued suggestions regarding the manuscript, but I remain responsible for judgments and opinions expressed in the book—and for any errors in fact or interpretation.

☐ Table of Contents

□ Frank Lloyd Wright

One

A Revolutionary Test

In his late teens he saw forty men killed or injured when a state capitol wing collapsed because of faulty construction.

In his late twenties he changed the shape of American shelter with radical new houses, tailored to the size of man.

By his mid-thirties he had designed a big building in steel and concrete with innovations like glass doors and steel furniture. It lasted nearly fifty years—but he outlived it by nine years.

In his forties his Imperial Hotel successfully defied the Japanese earthquakes.

At sixty-five he renewed a burst of creative genius that lasted twenty-four years.

Nearly ninety, he designed a mile-high office building, great auditoriums, civic centers, and opera houses, some of which are just now being built.

Throughout his life he battled prejudice and misinformation, crusading for a truly American architecture. He survived great personal tragedies and harassment with dignity and humor and without becoming embittered or disheartened.

These are some of the highlights of the eighty-nine-year

life span of Frank Lloyd Wright, who set out deliberately to
be the world's greatest architect—and succeeded.

*   *   *

Frank Lloyd Wright was testing some thin columns he
had designed, which were called "revolutionary."

Photographers and newsmen watched with amazement,
and finally with awe, as the big crane continued to pile sand
and iron on a slender, golf-tee-shaped pedestal 18½ feet high.
Once again Wright was battling officialdom, in the spectacular way that he loved.

So the State of Wisconsin said that the columns for the
new S. C. Johnson and Son, Inc., building wouldn't hold up
a weight of six tons? On a chilly day in early June, 1937,
Wright had set up a test column in Racine, Wisconsin, invited newsmen, and vowed to pile on many times six tons.

Half a dozen young architectural students—apprentices
who helped Wright in his work—clustered around him at
the test site. They knew from the books that "the Master's"
test column defied the ancient laws of building, but Wright
seemed jaunty and undisturbed. Had the world's greatest
architect overreached himself this time with a design that
was too daring?

The column, only nine inches wide at the base, tapered
outward to one foot five inches at the top. "The books" all
said that a column must narrow toward the top, rather than
the bottom. Nor could the height exceed nine times the diameter of the base. Under such a theory, the Wright column
could be only six feet nine inches, but it soared to more than
eighteen feet. The top supported a broad platter several feet
across, and Wright planned a whole forest of 86 of these

columns to hold up the roof of the Johnson administration building. The Wisconsin Industrial Commission, which passed judgment on the safety of large buildings, had said the columns might not be strong enough, and Wright demanded a test.

Soon the test column, braced upright by four slanting pieces of wood, carried a ring of sandbags around its outer edge. The weight of the bags was already well past the critical six-ton mark.

"Pile on more," said Wright imperturbably. He was sitting a short distance away, his hands folded calmly on the head of his walking stick, a slight smile on his lips, and the hint of a twinkle in his eye. This was one stage performance he was going to enjoy right to the end.

Another ring of the gray sandbags was lapped over the top of the first one—and then another layer. And still the column held, under a weight of more than thirty tons. "Keep piling!" The word was passed to the loading crew. They poured in loose sand and chunks of scrap iron. Now and then Wright stood up to look at the column through field glasses.

Wright's apprentices, outwardly calm, were beginning to smile a bit. By this time the state officials had lost any enthusiasm they may have had for the test.

"There's sixty tons on top that column now," Wright was told. This was ten times as much as it was supposed to hold.

"Well, I guess that's enough," Wright replied. "Pull the column down."

A jerk of the crane that had done the loading crashed the column to the ground, where it could be examined to see how well it had survived the stresses. The apprentices joined the curious reporters and building experts in examining the column. They saw a heavy steel mesh, with concrete clinging to both sides of it. Wright called the method a sort of marriage between the two materials, with the steel mesh representing the "bone and sinew" of the union.

On a summer's day just fifty-one years earlier, when he was a husky, well-knit youth of seventeen, Wright had his first experience with the safety of columns.

"The State Capitol is falling down!" came the shout.

The massive roar of a collapsing building rooted the youth to an agony of attention. The floors inside the new north wing of Wisconsin's State Capitol were crashing down, carrying dozens of construction workers to injury or death.

Clouds of white lime dust billowed from the windows, and screams came from men trapped in the mass of rubble and wooden beams. Workers whitened like statues by the lime dust ran from the basement entrance of the structure, flailing with their arms as if still warding off the falling beams from their bloody faces.

Young Wright clung to the iron fence of the Capitol park, watching in horror. For a person destined even before birth for a career as an architect, this was a brutal and tragic lesson in how things can go wrong with building.

Firemen soon pushed through the gathering crowds to lead the rescue work. Near young Wright, the spectators suddenly scattered when someone pointed to a hand sticking out of the mass of fallen brickwork on which the crowd itself had been standing. A mangled human form was pulled from the reddened plaster and brick rubble, but it was too late. Against the building, Wright saw a workman hanging head downward from an upper window, his crushed foot pinned to the sill by a steel beam.

As he clung to the fence, too sick and weak to move from the spot, the lesson in building failure was burned into his mind so that he would never forget it during the more than sixty years that he practiced architecture. He dreamed about it for several nights and resolved that when it came his own turn to build, he would try his hardest not to risk the lives of workmen or occupants of buildings by poor design or careless construction.

Actually the collapse that killed or injured forty men that summer's day in 1886 was not the fault of the architect, but Wright did not know that at the time. The architect had designed the foundation walls so generously large that the contractor thought it would be all right to fill their centers with rubble instead of concrete. When the weight of steel beams and masonry of the upper floors was added, the walls below collapsed. This plunged the whole interior of the building into the basement.

Within the year the sturdy brown-haired youth got still another lesson in architecture when his nerve and daring were tested by clambering over ice-coated steel beams, nearly one hundred feet from the ground, on a University of Wisconsin building that was under construction. Wright had wanted to enter the University to study architecture. But the University at that time did not offer any such courses, so he settled for engineering. He helped to pay his way by working as a draftsman in the office of Professor Allen D. Conover, dean of engineering, who was also superintendent of buildings for the University. The study of engineering was actually a blessing, for Wright got the training in calculating stresses and materials that some architects never acquired at that time. In effect, he became both architect and engineer.

Science Hall was under construction. It was to be a tall square building in red brick, and the steel skeleton was already rising, scarcely a block from the frozen surface of Lake Mendota, which bordered the campus.

Wright had been entrusted with the task of designing some steel appendages at the tips of the big trusses of the main roof. Somehow, the workmen were unable to get them attached, and Professor Conover suggested that Wright could remove them and get them to fit better. Perhaps his real purpose was to teach his engineering pupil a lesson in designing more carefully.

It was the middle of winter, in the bitterly cold Wisconsin climate where the thermometer now and then slides to 20 or 30 degrees below zero. The disgusted workmen had left the plates hanging from the tips of the roof trusses by the few bolts that they had been able to attach.

The young engineer went fairly rapidly up the ladders from floor level to floor level, but when he came to the long, slanting trusses, which were to support the steeply pitched roof, he proceeded more cautiously. The beams were sheathed in ice, and a strong wind off the ice-covered lake made footing dangerous.

Just as in later life he never backed away from controversy, Wright was no quitter now in the face of danger. He inched his way up the latticework of the metal trusses, looking down now and then at the bare bones of the building's steel skeleton. The only things in place were the beams for the lower floors. At last he reached the top, nearly one hundred feet from the basement level, where the trusses met. Cautiously he unbolted the defective pieces of metal and dropped them with a ringing clang to the foundation below. Then, as carefully as he had come up, he inched his way back to the ground. But to the end of his life he never felt that the adventure was "educational."

Although he had been told ever since birth that he was to become an architect, young Wright did not look or act like one during his brief college days. Indeed, his meager training did not seem to indicate that he would amount to much in any field. Always sensitive to the fact that he was not tall, he made up for it by being strong and tough physically. Years of farm work, much walking and horseback riding, and later boxing, gave him a physique that was to carry him well for eighty-nine years. But he was still painfully shy with girls and had only one close friend among the boys of Madison, where he was growing up.

His height of five feet eight and a half inches gave him a well-knit frame, which he kept in shape. When he was over sixty, he got into a knockdown fight with a creditor and gave a good account of himself, even though his own nose was broken in the battle. Past sixty-five, he hopped to the controls of a road grader to steer it through the mud of a Wisconsin spring. Well into his eighties, he clambered around building construction sites, relishing the odors of wet cement and freshly sawed lumber as he mounted scaffolds or slanting planks, ducked braces, and disdained the aid of helping hands.

The mental development that caused him to be recognized early as outstanding may be a tribute to the gentle persistence of his school-teaching mother. His formal education was not impressive. Wright himself said he was at the University of Wisconsin a little more than three years, but University records, possibly incomplete, list him as being there just a little over a year and a half.

Less than ten years later, well before he was thirty years

old, Wright had begun designing the "prairie houses" that
were to revolutionize American home building. He brought
room height down to man's size, eliminated basements and
attics, opened the house to the outdoors, destroying the
"boxes within boxes" that had been the style.

By his early thirties, Wright had created the Larkin
building of Buffalo, half a century ahead of its time, for it
was the first big building to be fireproof, air conditioned
throughout, to have metal-framed glass doors and double-
glass windows, and specially designed steel furniture. The
architect, in fact, outlived his own steel and glass creation
by nine years. The building was designed, used fifty years,
and then torn down as obsolete, all within Wright's lifetime.

In his forties came the earthquake-proof Imperial Hotel
for Japan, plus a number of giant projects that never got
into the building stage either because of the economic
depression or because of the chill caused by Wright's personal misadventures. These "dream castles," in turn, were
followed by a green old age of huge productivity, spiced by
world-wide acclaim.

Two

"Honest Arrogance"

Like many another genius, Wright was full of self-confidence. "Early in life I had to choose between honest arrogance and hypocritical humility. I chose honest arrogance, and have seen no occasion to change," [1] he wrote—and it was quoted against him forever afterwards.

Does genius always have a touch of arrogance about it? In Wright's case at least, during his whole life he was the prophet of a new kind of architecture, and often he needed all the arrogance and skill he could muster, in his battles against tradition and conformity in architecture.

The sturdy stock of Welsh pioneers played a big part in Frank Lloyd Wright's mental as well as his physical inheritance. His grandfather was a man from Wales named Richard Jones, a maker of black cone-shaped hats, which he sold at county fairs, in the years before he led his young family across the ocean and to Wisconsin. Tall and dark-eyed, he would throw one of his hats to the ground and invite prospective customers to "stand on it" to prove its durability. On Sundays, equally aggressive, he wandered the countryside, preaching a Unitarian faith that did not sit well in devout Welsh ears.

He had married Mary Lloyd and, following the Welsh

custom, had joined her name with his, to become Richard
Lloyd-Jones. Tired of the hostile reception in Wales for his
fiery preaching, Richard Lloyd-Jones, his wife Mary, and
their seven children set sail for America. They went along
the Erie Canal, through the Great Lakes, and from Milwaukee by oxcart to the little settlement of Ixonia, some forty
miles west of Milwaukee. There the growing family—three
more children came later—farmed for six years.

Then the Lloyd-Jones family, reduced to nine children because of the death of one small daughter, moved on nearly
eighty miles to the west and began to spread out in the Wyoming Valley. It was good farmland, running down to the
banks of the Wisconsin River, just south of the village of
Spring Green. Friendly Indians were still in the neighborhood, roaming the steep hills on the trail of deer and small
game. Oak and birch trees covered the slopes. Outcroppings
of limestone rock jutted above the broad valley floor.

John, James, and Enos, the powerful, strong-minded sons
of Richard Lloyd-Jones, soon set up their own farms along
the edges of the valley—straw-thatched roofs for the stables,
as in Wales; rail fences of split oak; simple, sturdy farm-
houses of wood, with stone chimneys and fireplaces.
Thomas, another son, ran a mill, and Jenkin, the fifth, later
became a noted Unitarian minister in Chicago. The lilacs
and bouncing Bet that Richard Lloyd-Jones's wife planted
spread out along the Wyoming Valley roadsides, where they
can still be found.

Richard Lloyd-Jones kept right on preaching, just as his
grandson was later to keep on preaching the message of a
new kind of architecture. Mounted on his horse "Timothy,"
the crook of a stout walking stick hung over his left forearm
and his Bible under the same arm, he roved the countryside

on Sunday, proclaiming the family's old Druid motto of "Truth Against the World." His grandson recalled this motto again and again when the world seemed not ready to accept the truths that the architect sought to make prevail.

The fourth child, Anna, became a schoolteacher. "With a free stride like a man," [2] as her son later described her, she walked in good weather through fields and woods to teach in a one-room rural school. She rode a horse in bad weather. Like her son, she had dark brown hair, with a fine nose, dark, dreaming brown eyes, and what her son called a "good, brave brow." During the Civil War, as she was just growing into womanhood, she attended Milton Academy, some twenty miles southeast of the state capital of Madison, where she had a wood stove and cooked her own meals, as the other students did.

Shortly after the war, while Anna was teaching school, she met and married William Russell Cary Wright, a native of Hartford, Connecticut, who had begun a medical education, then switched to law, and was now both a preacher and a teacher of music, neither of which brought in much money. Anna was twenty-nine, and William Wright, a moody, poetical man, small of stature, was seventeen years older than his bride. They set up housekeeping in Richland Center, a county seat about twenty-five miles northwest of Spring Green.

Here Frank Lloyd Wright was born June 8, 1869. Anna Wright, confident that her first-born would be a son, was equally determined long before his birth that he should grow up to be an architect. Months before he arrived in the world, she cut out ten full-page wood engravings of old English cathedrals from an English pictorial magazine and had them framed in flat oak to hang on the nursery walls.

The birth of her son shifted Anna Wright's attention from her husband to the baby, and the father felt the change. Within three years William Wright accepted a call to a church in Weymouth, Massachusetts, so the young family, now grown with the addition of a daughter Jane, went east. Here Anna Wright encountered the second major architectural education tool for her son. On a visit to the Philadelphia Centennial Exposition in 1876, she saw the new Froebel educational toys for children—strips of colored paper and structural figures to be made with small straight sticks and joining knobs.

With these came smooth maple blocks for building, which gave the boy Wright the feeling of textures, as well as form. Triangles of cardboard, colored an exciting scarlet, piqued the boy's imagination when they formed geometric shapes spread out on the table. He learned as much through his hands as he did with his eyes, feeling the smoothness as well as the shape.

It was also at the age of seven that the future architect got his first taste of complete exhaustion in pursuit of the arts. But it was the father's pursuit that wore out the child. William Wright loved music. He excelled on the piano and organ and taught his son to play acceptably, with the aid of much knuckle-rapping by pencils. But it was at the organ that the growing boy had his worst sessions. Beethoven and Bach were the father's favorites, as they were later the son's. While the elder Wright played, young Frank had to pump the bellows to provide wind for the organ pipes. After one rugged session, when the father played dreamily on until the son collapsed, thus stopping the music, Anna Wright put restraints on the playing.

Yet the music played a part too in the architectural

training. Wright taught his son to see a symphony as an edifice in sound. All his life the younger Wright kept up his love of music. As a boy, lying upstairs in bed, he memorized the pieces his father was playing at night on the old square Steinway piano. The architect later insisted that each of his own children had to master a musical instrument. Even at a time when he had no money or prospect of getting any, he would not hesitate to order a concert grand piano, trusting that somehow he could stall off demands for payment until he could unearth some cash.

Tiring of the hard-scrabbling life of a small-town minister, William Wright and his family returned to Wisconsin, where he set up a "conservatory of music" at Madison. Unfortunately, he did not gain much more money with this enterprise than he did at preaching. There was another mouth to feed, for a daughter, Maginel, had been born.

Some time after their return from the east, Uncle James Lloyd-Jones drove in the forty miles from Wyoming Valley, with a cow tied to the rear of the wagon, so that his sister and her children would have milk. A barrel of apples from the "Valley" had been for years a pleasant addition to the Wright larder, and now potatoes and other vegetables were being sent in regularly to help out the musician-father's income.

The powerfully built Uncle James, summoned by a letter from his sister that told of the family's financial troubles, was a strong contrast to the thin boy who stood before him at the Madison house one April morning. The tall farmer had a shock of wavy brown hair and a big brown beard that covered most of his face. When he laughed, his eyes crinkled to narrow slits—and he seemed to be laughing most of the time. The boy liked him immediately.

Eleven-year-old Frank was short and skinny, but at least he was now looking more like a man. Only recently his mother, weeping as she did so, had finally cut off the long golden curls that fell to his shoulders. Curls of that length were not uncommon on boys, but Anna Wright had probably kept them on her son longer than was customary. The boy's arms and legs were thin, his chest narrow. He did not realize what a rugged life he was about to embark on as he took Uncle James's hand and climbed into the wagon for the day-long drive of forty miles back to Spring Green. "Going to make a farmer of you, my boy," [3] Uncle James said with a hearty laugh.

The sharp rapping on the stovepipe that ran up the wall of his whitewashed attic room at the farm woke young Frank each morning at four o'clock, and he would wearily pull on his "hickory" shirt, blue overalls, cotton socks, and rawhide boots to go and help milk the cows. His arms and legs ached, and his back felt as if it would break. Uncle James's warm, confident voice and jolly laugh helped to keep up his spirits.

The boy learned to hitch up Pontius and Pilate, the big draft horses—and once he had a wild ride, clutching the harness of Pontius and bumping against the horse's legs just ahead of the murderous harrow, when the team ran away.

The discouraged city youth ran away twice himself, when it seemed to him that his aching arms just couldn't endure one more milking. Each time he was found, tearful and dejected, and persuaded by Uncle James or Uncle Enos, his mother's youngest brother, to return. Showing his ironlike arm muscles, Uncle Enos told the boy that his own would be like that soon if he kept up and declared, "Work is an adventure that makes strong men and finishes weak ones." [4]

But the young Frank thought of it as "adding tired to tired," and the care of horses, cows, pigs, sheep, and chickens seemed endless. However, the words of Uncle Enos, echoed by the equally powerful Uncle James, eventually did come true. He found that work could be an adventure when you were fit for it.

He was learning how an imaginative person can manage to endure monotonous tasks. All such work, he discovered, has its own rhythms, and if one can discover these rhythm patterns, the work can become passable, if not interesting.

Nevertheless, he loved to get away, when he could, to play in the small stream near the farmhouse, where he made dams, floated sticks, and even used his boots as a toy boat. There were excursions in the wagon now and then with Uncle James, going to Spring Green by way of the ferry. He wanted to know how the ferry worked, and he bombarded his uncle with dozens of other questions all the way over and back, while his brown legs kicked impatiently under the wagon seat. He hunted eggs in the stolen nests of the chickens, went for the cows through the dappled sunshine of the oak woods, and took his turn at the rugged work of teaching calves to drink from a pail.

Sundays were different. The boy's task, with horse and wagon, was to get quantities of flowers and green boughs to decorate the little wooden chapel in the Valley, where the Lloyd-Jones husbands, wives, children, and hired hands could turn up an audience of about seventy-five. There were hymns, often in Welsh, and preaching that was intended to— and did—bring tears to the eyes. "The luxury of the Lloyd-Joneses," Wright reflected later, "was not laughter, but tears. Until you had water in the eyes of them you really hadn't got them." [5]

And then there were Sunday picnics, starting with a simple plan for "a little graham bread, a little cheese, a drink of milk," and winding up instead with roast chicken or turkey, boiled ham, hard-boiled eggs, many kinds of pastry and rolls, preserves and pickles, and a multitude of cookies and cakes.

Every spring and summer, for four years, from April to the middle of September, young Frank worked on his uncle's farm, developing a rugged physique, plus a deep love of woods, valleys, earth, and all growing things. While he did not often copy these forms of flowers and plants in his later architecture, the patterns of simplicity and harmony powerfully influenced the kind of buildings he was later to design. They were not variations of trees and flowers, but they were all anchored as part of the earth, seeming to grow from their surroundings. He took the flaming red of the field lilies, for instance, for the "red square" that later became his mark in the lower right corner on all drawings.

Young Frank's farm experience came at a time when, some conservationists think, there was the greatest amount of game and wildlife that this country has ever seen. The reason for it was the split-rail fence, which zigzagged over the landscape, giving abundant corners where quail and other birds could nest, and rabbits, skunks, and weasels hide. Most boys would have been hunting enthusiasts with all that game at hand. Young Wright, however, looked at the colors and shapes of flowers with an artist's eye and had none of the hunter instinct.

"Has anyone sung the song of the patient, calf-bearing, milk-flowing, cud-chewing, tail-switching cow? Slow-moving, with the fragrant breath and beautiful eyes, the well-behaved, necessary cow, who always seems to occupy the choicest ground anywhere around?" [6] he wrote later.

He was mindful too that barbed wire was changing the face of America, just as it was replacing rail fences. "Someone should do the barbed-wire fence in song and story," he said. "It would be the story of the march of our later civilization. Together with the tin can, has it made man's conquest too easy?" [7]

Winters at the Second Ward school in Madison were not especially happy times. Schoolmates nicknamed him "Shaggy" in tribute to his great mass of unruly brown hair. In spite of his best efforts with brush, comb, and scissors, the nickname stuck for years.

Young Wright was desperately shy at school parties, being clumsy and tongue-tied in the presence of girls. And he developed few friends among the boys. His closest pal was red-haired Robert Lamp, whose legs had been crippled in childhood and who went about on crutches. A schoolyard rescue of "Robie" Lamp from his tormentors led to their friendship.

The two boys dreamed up dozens of mighty projects for building, salesmanship, and creation—in between bouts with tattered dime novels, which were inevitably found and confiscated by their parents. The passion of the boys for invention led them to make a water velocipede, a crossbow, bobsleds painted in gay colors, kites, water wheels, and other devices, some never completed.

Their longest hours, however, were spent over a small printing press with seven fonts of type, which they first set up in the old barn near the lake but later moved to the Wright basement. All his life, Wright was to sniff the smell of printer's ink. Occasionally he was the victim, cruelly "written up" when the misadventures of his private life were magnified by unscrupulous editors to sell papers. But during most of his life he used the press for his own purposes, expounding his unorthodox views on architecture, jabbing at unsightly buildings, kindling the imagination of the public with a sizzling phrase or an apt appeal to the sense of beauty.

As always, there was strong emphasis during those school years on music. Evenings were gay times around the old square piano, when girl friends or sisters of the boys would come in, and the lyrics of Gilbert and Sullivan turned the "concerts" into happy riots.

All the time, in unobtrusive, skillful ways, Anna Wright was encouraging her son in the direction of architecture. He was trying his hand now at designs. Anything capable of being constructed caught his eye. Bridges and dams were the reigning favorites, but the field was growing.

So, also, was trouble between son and father.

Three

A Job—and a Fight

"You'll do as I say!" William Wright shouted to his son as he marched the youth off to the stable. But the disciplinary scene did not end in the classical way. The years on the farm had strengthened Frank Lloyd Wright's body as well as his spirit. When the musician and preacher tried to "give a thrashing" to his son, the son promptly wrestled his father to the floor and would not let him up until the father promised to let him alone henceforth.

White-faced and shaken by what he had done, the youth went into the small house and told his mother, saying in excuse that his father should not try to do such things to a son who was nearly sixteen.

Matters had not been going well for some time in the little house by the side of the blue lake. The father's "conservatory of music," set up when the family returned from Massachusetts, had attracted very few of the 25,000 or so residents of Madison. The city had a big assembly room for musical concerts, but it was visiting musicians, not local talent, whom the people came to hear. They walked over board sidewalks or rode in carriages over unpaved streets rutted by farm wagons. Nor were there many pupils at the Wright conservatory. Some engagements to preach came along, but these also were rare.

The cow and the fruit and vegetables sent in by the Lloyd-Joneses of the "Valley" helped the family to survive, but they were bitter medicine for the father's pride. Now and then he noticed that his wife was holding back at the dinner table. She was eating less, so that there would be more for young Frank and for the two girls, Jane and Maginel. And the Lloyd-Jones family dropped strong hints now and then about the manner in which they thought "Sister Anna" ought to be provided for.

The pressures from his wife's family doubtless increased the chasm that had been opening between William Wright and his wife. One day, using the formal "Mister" she always employed when talking to him or about him, Anna Wright said:

"Well, Mr. Wright, leave us. I will manage with the children. Go your way. . . . If ever you can send us anything, send it. If you cannot we will do the best we can." [1]

The long succession of failures—as preacher, teacher, musician, and perhaps also as parent, had eaten away at the marriage of eighteen years. Doubtless William Wright's withdrawal in later years into his own intellectual world of books and music had their effect too.

Without a word, he stepped to the hatrack, picked up his hat, and walked out of his family's life forever. The marriage was quietly dissolved by a divorce, then considered a "disgrace," and Anna Wright bowed in shame at the constant reminder that she was a "divorced woman." She had not really believed that William Wright would take his hat and accept her invitation to leave. Until he died fifteen years later, she always thought that some day he would return.

Young Frank had entered the University of Wisconsin to study engineering because there was no money to send him away to an architectural school. He went to classes in the morning, walking the two miles from his home, then ate his sandwiches at noon in the office of Professor Conover. He spent the afternoons as a draftsman in Conover's office. Evenings, naturally, had to be reserved for study for his classes.

The collapse of the State Capitol wing had occurred while Wright was attending the University. It was also while he was working in Professor Conover's office that Wright had the experience of climbing the icy beams of Science Hall. Aside from a freshman dance and joining a fraternity, Wright had little social life at the University. He buried himself in books like Viollet-le-Duc's *Dictionary of Architecture*, which profoundly influenced him, and Victor Hugo's *Hunchback of Notre Dame*, which had a stirring chapter on the architecture of the famous cathedral.

He turned over in his mind Hugo's statement that the Renaissance was actually a sunset rather than the dawn of a new architectural era. As Wright considered this further, he came to feel that the time was ripe for a new spirit to lead the world forward. It would not be many years before he was convinced that he himself had been called by destiny to breathe new life into architecture.

Wright worried over the family's wretched financial situation and was uninspired by any of his teachers. He was sure he was wasting his time. Again and again he pleaded with his mother to let him go to Chicago, where he could be employed in some architectural office. Finally, at her son's insistence, Anna Wright wrote to her brother, Jenkin Lloyd-

Jones, famous Chicago Unitarian minister, who was then building a big new church on Chicago's south side.

"On no account let the young man come to Chicago," Uncle Jenkin wrote back. "He should stay in Madison and finish his education. That will do more for him than anything else. If he came here he would only waste himself on fine clothes and girls." [2]

The letter bolstered the views of Anna Wright but merely infuriated her son. He determined that he would go to Chicago, anyway, but vowed not to see his uncle or mention his name in getting a job. "I'll show him!" was his attitude, but he did not tell his mother of his plans.

To get money for his assault on the big city, Wright pawned his father's leather-bound sets of Plutarch's *Lives* and Gibbon's *Decline and Fall of the Roman Empire.* He even pawned the mink collar of his overcoat. After buying the railroad ticket, Wright had just seven dollars in his pocket when he boarded the train for Chicago, a few days after the letter from his Uncle Jenkin. He had given his mother a pretext that he would be staying at a friend's house for a day or two.

Chicago, in that late spring of 1887, had long since recovered from the effects of the great fire of sixteen years earlier and was exuberantly completing the transition from wood to stone buildings. It was an exciting, almost overwhelming place for a youth from a small city, but Wright approached with supreme self-confidence and enthusiasm.

He blinked at his first sight of electric lights—the garish blue arc lights that sputtered and flared at street corners. Seventy cents, a full ten per cent of his capital, went for the first night's dinner, and a dollar for a seat later at a ballet performance—which he did not find particularly good. With amazement he stood on the center span of a turntable bridge over the Chicago River and watched a tug and big ore boat go through. He rode a streetcar all the way to the carbarns and took another back.

Up early in his cheap hotel the next morning, Wright got a city directory and made a list of the architectural firms he wanted to call on. He walked through the gridiron of streets, dodging the big brewery wagons rattling over the cobblestones. He looked at the horsecars this time but did not ride because he wanted to hang onto the money that was left. Far from being thrilled by the sight of the big buildings, he was horrified by their cheap, uninteresting appearance. Walking past one tall building, he decided that it was a "thin-chested monstrosity" and promptly crossed its architect off his visiting list. Now and then the youth passed whole blocks of vacant lots, surrounded by high board fences, and he thought they were more attractive than the buildings.

Pretty soon, the college "toothpick" shoes he was wearing began to pinch, but Wright plowed on, crisscrossing the city and going extra distances because he had not thought of grouping the offices by location. After breakfast his total capital had been reduced to three dollars and ten cents, so he was not buying rides. At each office the story was the same: "Got any work for an engineer and draftsman?"

Some smiled at the unruly mass of brown hair atop the youth's head, so far from the current fashion. At two or three places he was told to come back "in a few weeks," or even months, which was small comfort for a person with three dollars and ten cents in his pocket. At one place he was astonished when a gray-haired architect asked him whether he had any drawings to show. It had not occurred to Wright to bring any to the offices. Fortunately, he had some in his bag, still checked at the railroad station.

Although his bones and his feet ached from the long day, he was not at all discouraged. Like many another youth down through the ages who has tackled the big city on an empty pocket, he was supremely self-confident. At a bakery near the hotel, he invested twenty cents in the kind of rolls and sweetmeats that had been rarities at home and persuaded the hotel clerk to move him to a cheaper room, costing only seventy-five cents a night.

The next day, sure that someone would engage his services, Wright strode forth again to conquer the city, after buying ten cents' worth of bananas. He ate them as he walked along, and they were to be his entire food for the rest of the day. Again, it was the same story: polite interest but no work.

Three more offices, visited on the fourth day, on a totally empty stomach, brought him to the end of his list of architects, and still no job. One place remained—the office of J. L. Silsbee, architect for the church then being built for his uncle Jenkin Lloyd-Jones. Wright had avoided Silsbee. Still stubbornly determined not to trade on his family name, Wright went to Silsbee's office, feeling sure that the architect would not know that he was the nephew of a client.

Cecil Corwin, a tall, bearded youth with a shock of wavy hair on his head similar to Wright's, met him at the door of Silsbee's office. Soon Wright learned that Cecil also was a minister's son and likewise interested in music. Wright, who had always needed a close companion, had found someone to replace Robert Lamp, the crippled Madison boy.

Silsbee, a tall, disdainful man with gold eyeglasses attached to a long gold chain, took a casual look at Wright's drawings and ordered him hired as a tracer—at eight dollars a week. The pay was much less than Wright had expected, but by that time he was so glad to get the job that he did not really care. When Corwin learned that Wright was down to twenty cents and had not eaten for more than a day, he took him out for a big lunch of corned-beef hash. The city, Wright felt, had been conquered—and he had a new respect and love for corned-beef hash.

Wright went to Corwin's home that night, and there Wright wrote to his mother, borrowing ten dollars from Corwin to send to her. It made him feel that at last he was repaying some of the cost of his early care. The next day the two youths visited the church being constructed for Wright's Uncle Jenkin. The minister was there and told Wright that his mother had been worrying about him.

From then on, Wright swung easily into a pattern of hard work and quick learning. Silsbee was a master of design, of the "pretty picture," which he could do rapidly in bold free-hand strokes. Wright quickly learned the technique, soon rose in pay to twelve dollars a week—and quit when Silsbee refused to make it fifteen. Wright tried another office but found he was being pushed too fast for his skill. He was expected to turn out drawings that he had not yet learned how to produce. With a sudden decision, he went humbly back to Silsbee and was rehired.

Architectural offices such as those Wright was working in were still in the phase of having a "designing partner" who drew the perspectives or "pretty pictures." After that it was up to the engineering partner to try to translate these pictures into a workable floor plan and construction details.

When the architect later became responsible for both floor plan and "picture," it was a big step forward in getting better buildings.

The turning point in Wright's architectural career came a few months later, when he was nearing twenty. A friend in Silsbee's office learned that the great Louis Henri Sullivan, who was among the three or four most promising architects of the Middle West, was looking for someone to do the interior drawings for the massive Auditorium theater and hotel that Sullivan had designed. Wright dashed over to the Adler and Sullivan office and was told by Sullivan to prepare some sample drawings of architectural decoration.

Sullivan—to the end of his days, Wright called him Lieber Meister, his "dear master"—was a small man, a trifle shorter than Wright himself, and always immaculately dressed. What impressed Wright from the first was the depth and penetration of his big brown eyes, flashing above a neatly trimmed brown beard. They seemed to bore through Wright and expose his inmost thoughts. Sullivan smiled rarely and could lash out savagely at a workman whose drawings did not come up to the Sullivan standard.

Architectural offices in the late 1880's in Chicago—or anywhere else—did not coddle the low-paid help. The master architect would gaze at a drawing, and if he did not like it, would indulge in a violent outburst. The "help" expected this and bowed to the storm, even though it was a bitter pill for a rising young draftsman to be singled out for a loud-voiced attack. Sometimes the humiliated draftsman would seize his drawing instruments and quit.

Fortunately, Wright had not been standing still during his year and a half in Chicago. From the library of his uncle's church he had drawn a book by Owen Jones, *Grammar of*

Ornament, as well as Viollet-le-Duc's *Habitations of Man in All Ages.* Where another designer might have been content with reproducing a few of the ornament drawings, Wright got a full hundred sheets of tracing paper and laboriously copied drawings until he had filled up every sheet.

Part of the secret of his genius lay in this willingness to do great quantities of hard, painstaking work. A few years later he would sit up nights lettering phrases and statements that he admired from Walt Whitman and Emerson. The lettering helped to sink the expressions deeply into his bones and, at the same time, improve his skill in draftsmanship. Sullivan also was an admirer of Whitman, and during the six years Wright was associated with him, this literary taste was another of the bonds of affection and comradeship that bound the two men together.

For two nights in succession after meeting Sullivan, Wright sat up until three in the morning, producing styles like Sullivan's, imitations of Silsbee, and some of his own creations. It was another example of the capacity for strenuous work that formed the background of his genius.

The imitations of Sullivan's own work were so outstanding that Sullivan at first believed they were tracings. Wright was promptly hired, at a rate of pay now up to twenty-five dollars a week, though he felt sure afterward that he could have started at forty. Soon he had a private office next to Sullivan's and was directing a crew of thirty draftsmen. They were preparing the massive amounts of drawings necessary for the interior of the Auditorium, which had a theater seating 4,000—big in any age. Wright was growing, under the eye of a master architect, for Sullivan was known later as the "Father of the Skyscraper." When Sullivan designed the Wainwright building for St. Louis, often called the first real

skyscraper in America, he boasted that he drew the plan in
just three minutes—which meant that he had it in his head
for a much longer time. Through Sullivan, Wright was ab-
sorbing the knowledge that the older man had acquired
during his four years at the Beaux Arts Academy in Paris
and his grasp of the new principle of the skyscraper. Wright
gloried in the fact that he was the highest paid draftsman in
Chicago.

"I became a good pencil in the Master's hand," [3] he explained later, paying tribute to the tremendous influence
Sullivan had on him.

But the books on architecture had not been the only thing
that Wright was experiencing at his uncle's church—when
he wasn't going to concerts with Cecil Corwin. One of the
activities was a costume dinner and dance, based on Victor
Hugo's *Les Miserables*, for which Wright appeared in
magnificent shiny black boots, scarlet military jacket, gold
braid, and a clanking sword. The weapon kept getting in his
way when he danced, but he would not give it up for anything.

During an intermission, when he was dashing across the
dance floor to join another group, he ran head on, literally,
into an attractive young red-haired girl named Catherine
Lee Tobin. Their foreheads met sharply, and both were
knocked to the floor.

The acquaintance thus begun so spontaneously soon rip-
ened into close friendship. Catherine, only sixteen, ruled her
own household as the favorite and oldest child. Wright became a frequent Sunday dinner guest, and Catherine always
saved a seat beside her in church for him. They took long
walks together, read books, and did all the things that young

people find to do which keep them together and soon make them feel that they are indispensable to each other.

Cecil Corwin tried to argue with Wright, pointing out that Catherine was very young and Wright not much older. He suggested that his friend go out with other girls, so as to get more perspective, rather than to drift into a life partnership with the first young lady he had taken out more than a few times.

Wright's mother, who had come down from Madison to live near her son, pleaded that he was being unfair to Catherine. "Have you thought of the consequences to this young girl of your singling her out to the exclusion of all others?" [4] she asked him.

The courting fever died down a bit then, aided somewhat when Catherine's alarmed parents sent her to relatives in northern Michigan for a few months, but it was renewed in full vigor when she returned.

Wright, meanwhile, got into more violent controversy at the office. The other draftsmen noticed from the beginning that Wright was a favorite of Sullivan's, and they began teasing him in small ways, behind the back of the foreman. They twitted him about his hair, still overlong, and his style of dress, which was too individual to suit them. Now and then his work would be deliberately interfered with. The group—half a dozen husky young men—used to go into a back room at noon to eat their lunches and engage in a few rounds of boxing. Wright could see that he would soon have to run their gauntlet and decided to outsmart them. He went to a Frenchman who conducted a boxing and fencing school and arranged to take boxing lessons every day for two weeks.

At the very first lesson the "professor" rocked him to the heels with a blow, which convinced Wright that he badly needed training skill for his arms and hands, even though he was rugged enough to take punishment.

A blond-haired conceited youth named Isbell was the first one at the office with whom Wright put on the gloves when he finally challenged the nagging group. Wright found Isbell's prominent nose a glorious target. Isbell began getting the worst of it, and his friends tried to end the encounter, but Wright was now fired up. When Isbell retired to nurse his battered nose, another member of the group promptly took his place, trying to wear out Wright.

After considerable wild swinging on the part of both, Wright lost his head, threw away his gloves, and demanded that they fight with bare fists. The gang didn't want this, and the fight broke off—but it did not clear the air. The persecution kept on, changing from nagging to outright enmity. A heavy-bodied, short-legged youth named Ottenheimer, full of jibes and taunts, was their ringleader.

"You're just a Sullivan toady anyway, Wright. We all know it," [5] he sneered to Wright one noon when the two were alone, except for a third youth. Thus challenged, Wright decided that the time had come to settle accounts.

He struck Ottenheimer full in the face, too excited to notice that the other man was wearing glasses. Ottenheimer fell and the glasses were smashed, but fortunately did not cut him or injure his eyes. With a savage scream, Ottenheimer grabbed an architect's long scratcher-blade knife and lunged at Wright.

Wright seized Ottenheimer's head under his arm in a wrestler's chancery hold, but Ottenheimer held the blade aloft and stabbed repeatedly at Wright's neck and shoulders. Wright finally threw him backward against a door.

Blood was running down his back and legs and into his shoes as Wright watched Ottenheimer struggle to his feet and prepare to attack him once more with the knife. Then Wright seized the T square from his desk and swung it by the handle, catching Ottenheimer in the side of the neck. The head of the T square broke off and flew to the other end of the room. Ottenheimer dropped like a poled ox and seemed lifeless. Anxiously, Wright and the other young man threw water on Ottenheimer until his eyes opened.

"I'll pay you for this, Wright!" [6] Ottenheimer threatened as he slowly struggled to his feet. Then he gathered up his drawing instruments and went out. Wright never saw him again, but he carried the welts of the knife attack on his back and neck for the rest of his life. A doctor found that all eleven stab wounds had driven to the bone, but fortunately none had penetrated the spine. The battle at least ended the gang's nagging attacks on Wright.

The "battle of the sexes" was still going on while Wright was having his difficulties establishing himself in Sullivan's office. In spite of the arguments of his mother, and of Catherine's parents, Wright and Catherine pressed steadily on toward marriage.

When he was just turned twenty-one and she was not quite eighteen, they were married on a rainy day by Wright's Uncle Jenkin in the church. It was wet all over. Anna Wright fainted during the ceremony. Catherine's father burst into tears, and even Uncle Jenkin was seen to wipe away some suspicious moisture from his eyes.

Wright had determined to design and build his own house

and arranged a deal with Sullivan to finance it. He agreed to work for Sullivan for at least five years, and the money to pay for the house was to be taken from his wages. The young architect had fallen in love with a plot of ground in Oak Park, a suburb at the western edge of Chicago, which had a wilderness of trees and shrubs reminding him of the farm scenes in Wisconsin.

"Be sure and keep within the amount of money available," Sullivan warned Wright when he began his house. The money provided by Sullivan had purchased the land and left $3,500 over for the house construction. With carpenters getting ten dollars a week, and even a two-and-a-half-story house with ten bedrooms costing only six or seven thousand dollars, the money would provide a fair-sized home.

Wright promised, but the desire for "just the right kind of house" for his bride and himself was very strong. He wanted a studio drafting room for his own use, gay colored glass for some windows, a masonry wall to set off the building—and before the house was finished, he had exceeded the agreed cost by $1,200. He said nothing to Sullivan but paid off the extra amount as best he could in the next few years. It was a familiar building experience, shared by some Wright clients later—and by clients of many another architect.

Struggling to pay for the house, and for the babies that arrived soon to help fill it, Wright turned to designing houses for Sullivan clients, doing the work evenings at home.

Four

World's Fair "Disaster"

Wright had six busy and immensely important years in the inspiring Adler-Sullivan office. Under Sullivan's general direction he had taken over the job of embellishing the interior of the Auditorium hotel and theater as the "pencil in his master's hand."

Wright watched in admiration as Sullivan's partner, the heavy-set, black-bearded Dankmar Adler, engineer to the core, created the sturdy trusses that spanned the Auditorium's seating area. Not content with the engineering feat of a big theater auditorium in the center of a building, the owners increased Adler's problems by insisting on a banquet room to be carried on trusses above the ceiling of the theater.

Adler was a master of acoustics, and the Auditorium was from the beginning a superb place for the performance of opera. The engineer developed his own theories and ideas, because there was no known set of acoustical principles at the time. He produced a series of setbacks and baffles in the ceiling that carried and even amplified the sound toward the rear of the great hall.

Adler's genius with acoustics made it possible to fill the big hall with magnificent sound. An indication of the Audi-

torium's importance as a national architectural milestone
came when the incomparable Adelina Patti sang on the
opening night, December 9, 1889, before an audience that
included President Benjamin Harrison, Vice President Levi
P. Morton, and notables from Chicago and the rest of Illinois. Sullivan, for his part, let his creative pencil, through
Wright, inscribe a whole garden of decorations over the
proscenium and arches of the new theater. Ornament, rich,
intricate, seemingly growing right out of the materials themselves, covered the pillars and curves of the new building
like a vine enriching a trellis or arbor.

The Auditorium, in fact, represented the high point in the
careers of Adler and Sullivan. The World's Columbian Exposition held in Chicago in 1893 produced a complete rever-
sion to the classical in architectural style, all but burying the
new thrust toward an American architecture that Sullivan
had been initiating with the Auditorium, the Wainwright
building in St. Louis, and several other skyscrapers where
Sullivan was beginning to capture the possibilities of a new
form.

This 1893 Chicago World's Fair changed the taste of the
nation almost overnight. People came by the millions, were
entranced by imitations of classical Roman styles in which
the fair buildings were constructed, and demanded architecture like that when they got home. A series of accidents had
led to a complete surrender to the classical style.

"Make no little plans, they have no power to stir men's
blood," [1] was the famous statement of the mighty Daniel
Burnham. He was the respected Chicago architect who had
been named chief of construction for the fair, which of
course had to be planned two years ahead of its opening.
Unfortunately, just as planning was getting under way,

Burnham's associate, John Wellborn Root, who was to have been consulting architect and who represented the strongest voice against tradition, died. Uncertain of Chicago architects' abilities to handle the vast undertaking, Burnham had already engaged a group of New York architects to assist in the work. The New Yorkers, from firms steeped in the classical tradition, largely took over the planning and designing of the fair, and their drawings became a competition to see who could copy the ancient forms fastest and prettiest. They made big plans, but all were copies of classical forms.

"The damage wrought by the World's Fair will last from half a century from its date, if not longer," [2] Sullivan cried. His prophecy proved correct, for the beginnings of an American architecture, in buildings of Sullivan, H. H. Richardson, and Root, were smothered in a great wave of Greek temples, Roman baths, and classic arches.

Adler and Sullivan had only one building at the fair, but it was a masterpiece. Their Transportation Building, essentially what Sullivan called a "train shed," housed an exhibit of buggies, wagons, coaches, railroad cars, and other forms of transportation. At the center of its front was a great arch over the entrance doors, with a history of transportation in curved tiers of sculpture looming above the entry. The walls on either side of the great central opening were left undecorated, emphasizing the glory of the radiant entry arch.

Wright, Sullivan, and Adler were side-tracked as millions of Americans poured in to view the fair and then set off for home, to demand imitations of imitations of the old Greek and Roman forms. The chance the fair had to stimulate an architecture keyed to American landscape, ideals, and way of life was passed by.

By this time the Adler and Sullivan firm was settled in the

tower of the Auditorium, where Wright, not yet twenty-five, had his own private office and supervised thirty draftsmen in an adjoining room. Louis Sullivan, son of Irish immigrants and only thirteen years older than Wright, had grown attached to the younger man. Often they spent long evenings in the Auditorium tower, talking of Walt Whitman, one of Sullivan's enthusiasms, or arguing art and aesthetics. The lights of the big city twinkled below them, and in the distance the dark waters of Lake Michigan tossed in seeming echo of their ruminations.

Soon after the turnstiles of the 1893 Columbian Exposition had ended their clicking, a painful break between Wright and Sullivan occurred. Wright for years had been putting in overtime at night, working on houses for Adler and Sullivan clients, with Sullivan's approval. Then he started doing some for his own clients, and Sullivan was furious when he found out about it. Following a violent scene, Wright and Sullivan parted, not to meet again for many years.

Wright, still in his mid-twenties, was now on his own, in a world that had turned to classical imitations. He faced an uphill struggle to convince clients that a new kind of architecture, more suited to America, would be better for them. He also faced a country troubled with financial difficulties, because the Panic of 1893 had almost stalled large construction. Architects had to take part of their pay in stock in a new building, and often, because of bankruptcies and receiverships, the stock became worthless.

A tempting offer, which probably would have put Wright firmly in the classical camp, came at this time, just after the break with Sullivan. Edward C. Waller, an aristocratic individual who had become a friend of Wright's, invited Wright and his wife Catherine to have dinner with Daniel Burnham, chief planner of the Chicago fair. After dinner, the men went into the library, and Waller carefully locked the door, much to Wright's mystification. Then came the proposition: Burnham, or "Uncle Dan," as he was known, made a magnificent offer to send Wright to the Beaux Arts Academy in Paris for four years, to be followed by two years in Rome, after which he was to join Burnham's architectural firm. All expenses would be paid by Burnham, including those for Wright's wife and family. This was the way the education of bright young men was financed—by rich patrons—in the days before Rhodes and Fulbright scholarships.

Wright, embarrassed by the grandeur of the offer—but certain that he did not care to follow the kind of classical architecture that Burnham undoubtedly had in mind—sat silent, scarcely knowing what to say.

"Another year and it will be too late, Frank," [3] Burnham said, trying to spur a favorable decision.

But Wright said it was already too late. He declared that Sullivan had regretted some of his years at the Beaux Arts. He asserted that copying Greek temples was not creative at all. With clear eyes, he saw that under Burnham's guidance he could be certain of an assured future of great financial and professional success, but he turned it down, choosing instead to develop his own style and to fight the uphill battle for clients and fame. For a young man in his twenties to reject such an offer was unheard of, but Wright did it. He chose the hard road because there burned within him the feeling that America needed a new kind of building and that he was the man to create this new type of structure. Genius had set its goal already and would not be turned aside.

In the next thirty years Wright watched the country go mad over the classic style copies, but he himself remained true to his own beliefs that architecture must not be a copying of ancient forms but something growing out of the conditions and needs of the area where it was to be built. It should be "modern," meaning the best in beauty and structural skill that current thought could give it.

"Form follows function," a statement frequently made by Sullivan, troubled Wright. He could see that it was silly to design a Greek temple and then squeeze the functions of a library in among the pillars, which was just what architects of the classical school were doing. Sullivan's idea was to determine what the building was to be used for and then design a form for it that would express that use. Wright finally changed Sullivan's thought slightly and preferred his own version, that "Form and function are one."

He got a chance to put these principles into practice with his first client, after leaving Sullivan. The man was W. H. Winslow, of the Winslow Ornamental Iron Works, who had frequently been to the Adler and Sullivan office in connection with the iron work he did for Sullivan's buildings. There he met and knew Wright. When Winslow wanted a house, he asked Wright to do it. The dwelling was the first to show the beginnings of Wright's "Prairie Style," the flat planes, closeness to the ground, sheltering roof, and harmonious treatment of the upper story.

Instead of a Queen Anne front, with a tower at the corner and "gingerbread" all over, Wright determined to make the form of the house follow the uses to which it would be put. He built it to the size of man, not to some mythical giant, and he intended it to indicate shelter and comfort, rather than a drafty castle suited to repel knights in armor.

The Winslow house was followed by dozens in the next few years in which Wright perfected his Prairie Style of horizontal line and flat plane, the welding of building to its site, rather than whipping up imitations of old English and French houses.

After the break with Sullivan, Wright had set up an office with Cecil Corwin in the fairly new Schiller building, for which Wright had been largely responsible while Sullivan was enjoying his new-found vacation spot in Louisiana. In that office Wright introduced for the first time in America the clear plate-glass entrance door, enclosed in a wooden frame. He and Corwin did their own lettering of names on the door's plain glass and then called in a technician to apply the gold leaf to the names. They shared a common reception room and stenographer but were not partners.

Besides the plate-glass door, another Wright innovation came in lowering the ceiling of the reception room, putting lights above a ground-glass ceiling, and thus achieving a general bright illumination from overhead. The method is so common now that it is taken for granted, but when Wright began it, clients were dazzled by the "daylight" effect.

Experts on architecture can dispute as they will, but it is possible that one Wright limitation was also a blessing for home builders: he did not get commissions for big buildings but instead concentrated on houses. Loving the challenges of site and the varied needs of clients, Wright developed his Prairie Style of dwellings to a complete mastery of them, which would have been unlikely if he had been engaged in creating big offices or theaters. Had he concentrated on big buildings, he might well have suffered the fate of Sullivan and been ignored because he was ahead of his time.

It was Wright's family that suffered, rather than his style. The bitter truth for an architect is that to design houses is a luxury. Each one takes proportionately more time and brings in much less money than a commercial building. Indeed, Wright started on the design of homes simply because Adler and Sullivan wouldn't be bothered. The houses were given to Wright to do at home, for extra pay. When he started designing houses on his own, he soon discovered that the client was more demanding than was the man who wanted a store or office building. Much time was spent in conferring, cajoling, and changing. And then—there were women to please, which was not the case with an office building.

Here also Wright was well suited for the task. He was a striking and dynamic figure, with his curly brown hair, flashing blue-gray eyes, and rich, deep voice. He was slim, boyish, and handsome, and he had one further advantage as far as the ladies were concerned: with his height of five feet eight and a half inches, he was more nearly on eye level with them and thus did not seem to "tower" or dominate. His looks and his height, in fact, may well have been a major factor in securing commissions for enough houses to keep his growing family supplied with food and clothing.

The quip was as true in Wright's early days as it was later, that "the job of the architect is to design a house that will please the wife and which the husband can afford." [4] Wright's personal charm and warm sympathy toward women—perhaps a result of his close ties to his mother—may well have been deciding factors in getting many a house commission.

Whatever the combination of reasons, the lights burned late in the drafting room connected to Wright's home in Oak Park. He never emphasized it in his writings or his conversations, but the designs showed by their skill and completeness that many more hours went into them than could be accounted for by ordinary office schedules.

There always seemed to be money for the luxuries, like concerts, gay clothes for his wife, which Wright designed himself, for color prints, and flowers and books, but the necessities had to take care of themselves. Often they didn't, and Wright would be faced by a grocery bill, which once ran into several hundred dollars because it had accumulated for many months. He commented ruefully in later years that people were too ready to trust him for their pay, and so the bills mounted up.

Somehow he usually managed to find the money, getting advances on his salary from Adler and Sullivan or finding a new client after he had left the Sullivan firm, but it didn't always work. One time, the sheriff spent the night in the children's playroom, refusing to leave until Wright scraped up $85 the next morning for a long-overdue bill.

Wright and his lively young wife had scarcely been a year in the attractive house he had built, with the help of an advance from Sullivan, when the first of six children arrived. Curiously, neither Wright nor his wife had really expected this sort of increasing drain on the family finances. It couldn't be called a budget, because they both simply wrote checks until the bank sent them bounding back with big red ink marks indicating "not sufficient funds."

Although the children were a money burden, Wright turned to the job of being a good father with the same energy with which he attacked other tasks. He deeply loved his children and appreciated each one as a sturdy, unclassifiable individual. Was he making up for the lack of affection he had received from his own father? More likely, it was just his own warm, outgoing nature. Throughout his life he kept his spirits young by unfailing interest in the children of clients and friends, thinking of them as growing individuals in their own right, not just something to be shushed and sent away.

The architect's first child was a son, Lloyd, curly-headed, blue-eyed, and mischievous—as all the children were. After two years came John. In two more Catherine, the first daughter, arrived, to be followed by a son, David, two years later. Then, after another two years, a second daughter, Frances. Five years went by, and then Llewelyn, last of the children, was born, in 1903.

What romps and gay times Wright had with this growing brood! His architectural studio, added a year or two after the house was built, formed a second structure close to his home. In fact, a corridor connected the two buildings. Although he maintained an office in downtown Chicago, he liked to be able to work all or most of the night, if need be, when he was developing an architectural idea. In typical Wright fashion, a giant willow tree between home and studio was simply enclosed within the corridor, covering the two establishments from above with its greenery.

Down this corridor the children often scampered, sometimes to the embarrassment of Wright. One time little Catherine, her jaws working rhythmically with forbidden gum, sidled through the door while Wright was having a difficult first presentation of house drawings to a wealthy woman client. Catherine said her mother needed ten cents. Wright tried to shoo her off, but in a moment she appeared above him on the balcony, to renew her plea. But Wright couldn't fulfill it because at that moment he didn't have even a dime in his pocket.

Frances, the second daughter, was always finding and bringing home stray cats and dogs—and also had the ability to stand and wail at the top of her lungs when she was crossed. Son Lloyd was bewitched one Sunday morning by a whirling sprinkler and advanced upon it, in spite of his father's strict orders. Half-drenched, spluttering, and fighting mad, Lloyd kept on until he could put his hands on the sprinkler, which completely soaked him. The son was showing as much determination as the father when challenged by an obstacle. Just at this moment his mother, Catherine, returned from church, elegantly gowned, and saw her son apparently being half drowned. She rescued him, to the ruination of her own dress, and scolded her husband, who was laughing so hard at Lloyd that he could not even shut off the water.

Wright often worked late into the night on plans and drawings, but he was always ready to break off in the middle or especially at the end of the day for a frolic with the children. There were so many, and they ran around so fast, that even Wright got confused. Once a dinner guest friend seized a galloping child, held it up, and demanded that Wright name it. The architect missed.

Gas-filled balloons, great clusters of them, were a must for every party. One Christmas, Wright turned up with bicycles for all his youngsters who could ride. Each child had a musical instrument, also, on which he was expected to perfect himself.

Wright's wife Catherine had her hands full, a young bride swiftly become a mother, in coping with her growing brood. Wright himself, his brown curly hair agitated in a great mop on top of his head, was swimming in a sea of problems, trying to do enough work, at home after office hours, to close the financial gap for his growing family.

Five

The Man-Sized House

If the people who lived in the Chicago suburban houses of the 1890's had dressed like the architecture they lived in, the men would have sallied forth to work each morning in chain mail or a Roman toga, and their wives would have struggled to the grocery in farthingales and lace. The houses were miniature copies of Greek temples and other old styles that never were suited to American life. But scarcely anyone thought about breaking the chain, let alone wanting to do it, until Wright came along.

"Walk for a few blocks through the streets of our city where 'good copies' abound, and you will find a different civilization on every corner and subcivilizations aplenty in between—and yet nobody laughs!" [1] said Louis Sullivan.

Architect Wright watched Sullivan changing the concept of a tall building by the way he treated it as a skyscraper to emphasize height, rather than pretending that it was just an overgrown masonry building. Wright wondered whether the same sort of radical change could also be applied to the houses around him. He began to think of them as ugly boxes, divided inside into yet more boxes, and shut off and divided by doors and doors and doors. Everywhere you looked, there was a door or a wall right in front of your nose.

And when most men were less than six feet tall, "What is the sense of having ceilings twelve or even fourteen feet high?" he asked himself. Doors and their openings loomed way above the men and women who went through them. Windows were like small holes punched in the side of a box. Outside and inside, also, houses tried to look like something else than a dwelling. A brick wall might appear to be solid masonry but was more likely to be a thin shell almost literally pasted onto a wooden frame. Fake beams on the inside supported nothing and even had to be supported themselves from the ceiling. Windows were swathed in heavy drapes to keep out the light.

The Queen Anne style once popular in England was now a reigning favorite two hundred years later in America, among all the other styles resurrected from the ragbag of the past. It had an imposing front, usually with a tower or bulging group of windows. At the rear, the house dropped down to some low shacks for kitchen and woodshed, giving rise to the taunt, "Queen Anne front and Mary Ann back."

A typical home of a well-to-do family, besides the fourteen-foot ceilings, had a floor plan that was awkward, but the inhabitants did not mind because they had never seen anything better. The furniture appeared in bewildering variety because the catchword was to have something "unique." Thus each chair and table would be different. Black oak, carved with animal heads, was a favorite for chairs, and the umbrella stand could be solid brass or a black walnut "hallpiece" complete with mirror and marble top.

Grass cloth, burlap, or paper colored to look like leather sometimes covered the lower portions of halls and stairway walls. Varied dust-collecting objects brought back from European trips stood around on the shoulder-high shelves that circled some rooms. If the house did not boast a "Japanese room," at least it had a big vase or bit of statuary brought back by Far East traders. Openwork screens from Japan, heavy pieces of silver, and mahogany dining tables were the fashion.

Thinking of his own houseful of children, romping in a big playroom or racing through the corridor to the studio, Wright wanted to do houses that would help children appreciate beauty because they would be living in beautiful surroundings. Why not give both children and adults the dignity and luxury of living in the entire house, rather than shutting off parts for "company?" he reasoned. Let them have spaciousness and sunlight, he declared, along with a feeling of shelter and a sense of the outdoors, all drawn to human scale.

Americans, Wright decided, deserved an architecture based on their own upstanding character as free citizens in a democracy, rather than the outworn forms dragged across the ocean from Europe. First of all, man would be his measure for height, not some grandiose worship of castle-room dimensions. Accordingly, he cut down door openings to a little higher than the human figure.

Of course, if man was to be the measure, what better man than himself as a measuring stick? Picture him standing up from his drafting board, to his full height of five feet eight and a half inches, and declaring that this would be the new standard. Had he been six feet tall, the "human scale" of all his buildings would have been different, he conceded many years later.

The basement was the next to go. Wright had long felt that basements below ground level were "unwholesome," and besides, families had a tendency to throw their discarded furniture into them as a sort of perpetual junk heap, he decided. And what is the sense of having a house looking as if it were "perching like a bird" on a basement foundation sticking up a couple of feet above the ground, Wright reasoned. He moved the basement up to the first floor, designing it as a low masonry pedestal for the living quarters, which he placed on the second floor.

To cut down the height of the house, Wright also swept away the steep-roofed attic, whose dormer windows brought little light and air into the servants' quarters. It was an era when servants were cheap and plentiful. They worked in the kitchen and laundry in the basement and slept in the attic. When their living and working quarters were moved to the ground floor, it may have had an unintended effect: for the first time they were able to look out the windows onto a world at their own level, and they soon began to walk right out.

Nearly two generations later, when the "servant problem" had been solved by the scarcity and expense of servants, Wright moved the living quarters of his houses down to ground level, creating one-story houses where the housewife did practically all the work.

Wright was building on the flatlands of the Illinois prairies, and he wanted his houses to emphasize the horizontal line of the land on which they stood. He drew the emphatic lines of roof, window sill, and foundation parallel to the earth. He designed great flat walls, which were long rather than high, just like long strips of prairie sod set on edge. The "horizontal line and the flat plane," his tools to relate or "marry" the house to the ground on which it stood, often extended past either end of the house in the form of low walls or lines of planting, keeping the eye turned to horizontals.

Wright sharpened a fistful of pencils, both colored and black, and attacked the challenging plain expanse of white paper before him to perform other revolutions. Instead of a small hole poked in the center of a wall for a window, he made the windows a band of light right under the roof, sometimes running along the whole side of a wall. Often the windows turned right around a corner of the house, a thing unheard of then, giving the effect of the corner of the roof "floating" above the walls.

"I fought for outswinging windows because the casement window associated house with the out-of-doors, gave free openings outward. In other words, the so-called casement was not only simple but more human in use and effect. So more natural. If it had not existed I should have invented it," [2] Wright said.

As he experimented with new arrangements of windows (called fenestration), Wright began to think of them as a sort of luminous wall. Each house had its "dark side," he knew, because of the tendency of surveyors to lay out streets north-south and east-west, but Wright thought this could be changed by facing houses to the south, which he called the "comforter of life."

Plate glass was still new and expensive. The first machine for making electric light bulbs, instead of blowing them by hand, was invented in 1895. Wright could see great possibilities ahead for glass.

"This super-material glass as we now use it is a miracle," he would tell clients. "Air in air to keep air out or keep it in.

Light itself in light, to diffuse or reflect, or refract light itself." [3]

The little boxes within boxes—the separate rooms, halls, closets, dining, "drawing rooms," and music rooms—were also blown out or modified by the fresh winds of change. Why have the piano closed off, for instance, in a separate music room, or why set up a small cubicle as a parlor, in which to entertain the minister or some acquaintance for an hour or so once a week? What Wright wanted to create was a sense of free space within the interior of the house—a big living room blending into an entrance hallway, for instance, with low screens or subdivisions marking off areas for music or books. He wanted to give a sense of space, freedom, and unity to the whole interior rather than have a collection of boxes set apart from each other by doors or walls.

Wright still used partitions and doors in the bedroom sections of the house, but he succeeded in making the social rooms into a plastic, flowing unity where it was difficult to determine at what point one segment of the house began and another left off. The lower ceiling enabled him to use lower roofs, with less pitch than had been the custom. Sometimes, when the ceiling got near the outside wall, it turned into the slant of the roof and went on down to meet the tops of the windows.

Most pleasantly, the fireplace came back into the American home as a joy and comfort to the inhabitants. Some years earlier, when stoves and furnaces were developed, designers had changed the fireplace into a mere shadow—a strip of narrow marble for a mantel and a shallow opening beneath, sometimes containing fake logs or a gas jet. Wright not only restored the fireplace; he glorified it beyond what it had been for many a year. He created great masonry masses jutting out into the room, with ample opening for good-sized logs, and a hob or low seat of masonry at one side of the opening. Here someone who came in from a cold walk, or just wanted extra warmth, could toast himself almost on top of the fire. The faint but delightful odor of wood smoke from an open fire returned to homes to replace the rank smell of burning coal.

Instead of a forest of skinny chimneys rising above a roof, Wright made his chimneys broad and squat, scarcely appearing above the roof level. Thanks to central heating, his houses needed only one or two of these massive chimneys.

The walls and other building materials were different too. Wright wanted to get away from the falsities of construction that had crept into the building business. If brick or stone was to be used for a fireplace, let it show as itself, with good craftsmanship in the masonry, rather than cover most of it with a wood sheath. Windows and doors used to be boxed around their edges with heavy framing, often elaborately decorated with scrolls, flutings, and other evidences of the new woodworking machines, which could make almost any piece of wood look as if it had just escaped from a Greek temple.

Wright cut this fancy boxing down to a few plain strips of wood around the door and window openings. With similar thin, flat strips of wood, he divided walls and ceilings into large, harmonious panels, breaking up what would otherwise have been monotonous masses of plaster.

The new houses also called for a revolution in furniture. Out went the spindly curved legs of French and English copies, elaborately stained and waxed and decorated with silver or brass. In their place, Wright designed massive

tables that were built as part of the house, taking an irregu-
lar shape sometimes or being cut out to fit around a pro-
jecting part of a wall. Chairs sometimes tended to have more
geometry than comfort, but to make up for it, they carried
the eye into patterns that emphasized the straight lines of
wall and window.

"I have been black and blue in some spot, somewhere,
almost all my life from too intimate contact with my own
early furniture," [4] Wright confessed in his later years, but he
never ceased his attempts to design a better chair.

Another change: instead of high ceilings above the entire
room, like a great empty cavern looming over the floor,
Wright began to break his ceilings into two or more levels.
At one side of the room he would design a low canopy
effect, with a ceiling only a foot or so above head height.
The platform above gave a place for concealed indirect
lighting, to be reflected in diffused grace off ceiling and upper walls.

Architect Wright may also have remembered farmboy
Wright, the lad who went off with horse and wagon on Sunday mornings to get great limbs and masses of foliage to
decorate the Lloyd-Jones chapel in the valley near the Wisconsin River. The balconies or overhangs in the new houses
he built could be a resting place for branches cut from the
trees of vacant lots or masses of foliage from the nearby
roadsides. A big vase, a piece of sculpture, a gay piece of
cloth, could be the decoration in seasons when there were
no leaves on the trees or interesting weeds along the roads.

The visitor also got an unexpected lift of the spirit when
he came into a room with a two-level ceiling, usually with
the lower section over the principal entrance. First came the
warm, cozy feeling of the low-ceilinged space, and then, as

one stepped further into the room, the rest of the ceiling seemed by contrast to be even higher than it actually was.

When Wright thought of this new interior freedom of houses, he recalled Louis Sullivan's comment about the "plastic" nature of ornament and decoration. Just as Sullivan's rich flower and branchlike ornament seemed to grow out of the pillars of his rooms and spread naturally along walls and arches, Wright thought of his room designs as flowing like a plastic in a mold, from one room into another.

Photographers knew what he was talking about when they tried to pick out one section of a room to picture. They found themselves swinging their cameras almost in a circle, for each wall or a corner subtly merged into the adjoining architectural feature, so that it became difficult to know just where to stop the picture.

But the cameramen weren't the only ones having trouble. From the banker who furnished the money for a loan, through the contractor, the building material supplier, and the workmen who put the wood and stone together, there were complaints about the new simplicity that Wright was promoting. Like every innovator, Wright was walking a stony road, where the forces of reaction and love for the past tried to hold him back.

Perhaps the people who asked him to design houses for them had the hardest time. After the house was built, they would be living in it, subject to the jibes and ridicule of neighbors and friends, for this country has never been easy on the person who tries new things.

One client even came to Wright and asked him to design a traditional-style house, saying that he didn't want to go down side streets to take the train to the city every day because he didn't think he could stand the comments of his neighbors. Wright yielded to the man's request—not to save the man embarrassment, but because Wright desperately needed the money for his growing family. He boasted later that it was the only time he had compromised his principles. Actually it ended as an English house—with Wright style.

Bankers, by nature a cautious breed, declined to lend money on these new-fangled houses, so the client had to turn to friends to get his financing. Contractors who faced these unfamiliar designs and construction, which didn't follow usual patterns, would roll up the plans, hand them back, and simply decline to bid. Workmen, used to covering up sloppy work with the "trimming" that was splashed over corners and around openings, complained at Wright's rigid standards of construction. Sometimes an incompetent contractor ran the costs up so high that the client was faced with bills far larger than he had planned for, and this provoked hard feelings.

But actually the clients were not suffering. They knew their houses were built to human scale, not a castle fairyland, and were convenient, highly livable, and superbly fitted to the ground on which they stood. As one occupant put it: "The only trouble with living in a Wright house, really, is the fear that some day you may be forced to move. It is like living within a work of art."

Six

"Romeo and Juliet"

Like many another young person starting out in a new line of work, Wright had the best wishes of his close relatives— but not their full confidence. They expressed their doubts freely, every time he tried something new or different. A windmill was the unlikely subject that brought the impetuous Wright into conflict with his five gray-bearded Welsh uncles.

Aunt Ellen, usually called Nell, and Aunt Jane, the Lloyd-Jones maiden aunts who ran the Hillside Home School for youngsters in the Wyoming Valley, needed a windmill to pump water for dishes and baths and other things, but they wanted one that would harmonize with the soft lines of the hills. Could Nephew Frank do something more pleasing to the eye than the skeleton steel windmill towers that dotted the countryside's farmyards?

Wright sent the aunts a drawing of a radically new kind of tower, built of nails and boards rather than a braced steel frame. It was like an eight-sided barrel, with the staves nailed crosswise; only this barrel was to be sixty feet high. Cut into the windward side of the barrel was a diamond-shaped piece, also rising sixty feet. Wright named the windmill tower "Romeo and Juliet" and explained that barrel and

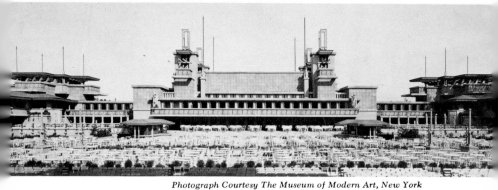

The Midway Gardens, Chicago (1914)

Courtyard and wing of the Imperial Hotel, Tokyo (1916-1922)

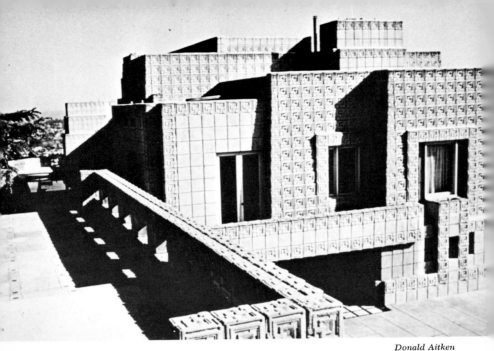

Charles Ennis concrete block house, Los Angeles (1924)

Taliesin East drafting room, with "abstract forest" of oak trusses

Edgar Tafel

Frank Lloyd Wright picnics in the Wisconsin hills

Apprentices gather around Frank Lloyd Wright at Taliesin East drafting board (1937)

Hedrich-Blessing

Mr. Wright and apprentices ponder a problem

The first "Usonian" house—the Herbert Jacobs house No. 1

Frank Lloyd Wright, in baggy pants and sandals, watches test of heating pipes for first radiant system

"Fallingwater" with cantilevered balconies flung over mountain stream near Bear Run, Pennsylvania (1937)

Test column for the Johnson Wax Co. building carries a sixty-ton load

Interior, Johnson Wax Co. administration building, Racine, Wisconsin

Mr. and Mrs. Wright chat with stage critic Alexander Woollcott at Taliesin East

diamond were necessary to each other—a "composition of forces," as the engineers call such things. The two would interact, transforming the violent push of the wind into a pull on the big iron fastener straps sunk into the heavy stone foundation at the base.

"That thing will blow down in the first big wind," Mr. Cramer, the Spring Green carpenter, told the aunts flatly. The five skeptical uncles backed him up, sure that "that boy" in Chicago didn't know what he was doing, even though he had then been dealing with architecture for seven years. The aunts telegraphed their doubts to Wright, who replied simply, "Build it!"

The five uncles, in solemn family conclave, were still opposed, but Aunt Nell, the lively and emotional half of the school, told them: "Does the boy want to build anything that will fall down any more than we do? He has even more at stake!" [1]

The young architect conceded that he had never seen exactly that same engineering principle carried out, but he added that he hadn't seen anything against it either. So up the tower went, with workmen scrambling to the ground on windy days because the tower swayed—as intended—several inches. When a fourteen-foot windmill wheel was mounted on the wooden structure, the uncles were convinced that this meant the end. They were sure no frail contraption of wooden barrels wedded to wooden diamonds could withstand the strong Wisconsin winds.

After each storm the uncles would come to their farmhouse doors to peer up, hand shading eyes, toward the hilltop where Romeo and Juliet literally held sway, but the tower outlived them all, as Wright had predicted it would. Pleased with their distinctive windmill, the aunts had their

nephew design big masonry school buildings for them—
which fell into disuse when the school closed. More than a
score of years later, Wright restored the buildings as a work-
shop and quarters for the young people who came to learn,
when he set up a "school" for architectural apprentices.

Some years after Wright showed how the ancient craft of
carpentering could be combined with unusual engineering
principles to build a striking windmill, he took an opposite
tack with a speech at Chicago's famed Hull House in which
he defended use of machines in creating human shelter. Architects and craftsmen had been bewailing the decline in
skills and asserting that the growth of machines, which
could endlessly duplicate designs in wood or manufacture
thousands of identical window frames, would ruin the creative arts and would spoil the looks of buildings. This same
idea was preached by William Morris, English poet and artist, but it did not halt the onward march of machines.

To the disgust of his fellow architects, Wright said that
the machine could indeed be tamed to be the servant of
man, instead of his master. The *Chicago Tribune* hailed
Wright in an editorial, but his fellow architects disagreed—
the first of a long series of disagreements over his methods
and the looks of his buildings.

Although Wright complained much in his later years that
he was "ignored" in America until long after he was ac-
claimed by foreign architectural experts, he got considerable
recognition both nationally and locally, in his home base of
Chicago, as the new century was beginning. The Hull House
lecture in March of 1901 had followed an article on his work
a year before that appeared in the *Architectural Record*, by
his friend, Robert C. Spencer, Jr. The *Ladies' Home Journal*,
in 1901, commissioned him to do a design for a Prairie Style

house, which the magazine printed—and promised its read-
ers could be built for $5,835. In 1902 about half the cata-
logue of the annual exhibit of the Chicago Architectural
Club was devoted to Wright's buildings.

The serious work of drafting went on days, and often
nights, but the lighter side of life was far from neglected.
Wright's son John recalled later that Wright would buy
colored gas balloons "by the dozen" and play with them by
the hour in the children's playroom. John Wright pictured
him with "brown eyes full of love and mischief, a thick pom-
padour of dark wavy hair. . . . His smile enlivened everything about him; his laugh defied grief and failure." [2]

One of the "toys" of the studio home was a player piano,
at which Wright would spend hours, his hands fondling the
throttles as he played Beethoven and perhaps thus got revenge for the many hours he had spent pumping the organ
for his father's playing. As the children grew older, they
were taken to the theater with their father, whose passion
for music was only equaled by his love of the theater.

"When in the theater, tam, stick and all, he would parade
down the aisle to his seat, pause—swing toward the audience, remove his cape—look right, left, up into the balconies like a Caesar about to make an oration—then he
would sit down," [3] John Wright recalls.

There was, of course, considerable of the theatrical flair in
Wright, as there often is in persons who seek to convert their
fellow man to new ideas. The specially designed clothes, the
Malacca walking stick, the unusual neckties—all helped call
attention to the message of the architect, just as a flourish of
trumpets keys the audience to a pageant. And Wright could
be affirmative in speech as well as dress. He astonished El-
bert Hubbard, the famous New York State editor, by telling

him that he intended to be the world's greatest architect, but Hubbard may not have been fully certain that Wright meant it seriously. Rabindranath Tagore, noted poet of India, who was only eight years older than Wright but had the beard and manner of a prophet, was one of several distinguished persons who visited the Oak Park home of the architect.

Wright was one of the first persons in the Chicago area to get an automobile when these new-fangled contraptions came along. It was a four-cylinder Stoddard-Dayton sport roadster, upholstered in brown leather, with a canvas top, brass trimmings, and a body enameled straw yellow. People in Oak Park called it the Yellow Devil, and police threatened at one time to confiscate it. When the architect got into the front seat to drive, he wore a linen duster and goggles. And when the eldest son Lloyd got his hands on it, he was promptly jailed and fined $100 for unauthorized driving. Son John, when he took his turn, managed to wreck the car, with a repair bill that ran to $350. Father and sons were immensely flattered when the manufacturer borrowed the car to enter it in an automobile race.

Not all the riding was done in cars. True to his love of the outdoors and the constant desire for exercise, Wright did a lot of horseback riding. Kano, a black five-gaited horse named after a Japanese nobleman, was Wright's favorite, but the children had horses too. There was Kit for John, Merrylegs for daughter Frances, and Gypsy, a western bronco, for Lloyd.

Neither the gay times with the children, the horseback rides, nor music and the theater could keep Wright from close attention to the way his houses were being built. Fred McCaddon, a plasterer, recalled nearly sixty years later the architect's passion for perfection and his sharp retorts when anyone crossed him. McCaddon worked on a house for Francis W. Little in Peoria, Illinois, which Wright did in 1901, and this is the way he looked to the workmen:

"Wright appeared on the job several times during construction. He was insistent on things being done the way he wanted and was quick with answers if anybody disagreed with him." [4]

In the middle of a succession of houses, great and small, Wright got a chance to try his hand at a big factory office building in Buffalo for the Larkin Company. He decided the time had come to make office buildings different from make-believe Greek temples, Roman villas, or petrified wedding cakes. This was the fashion that had swept the country after the Chicago World's Fair of 1893 had put an abrupt halt to a trend toward an architecture suited to American life. Wright wanted to do for business buildings what he had already done for houses—to create something that would fearlessly proclaim itself part of current American life, rather than be a copy of some imported foreign style.

Once again the horizontal line and the flat plane came into play, and Wright created a building that was constructed around a great roofed-over central court. Actually, the administration building was like a giant vault, sealed especially against the smoke of trains, which ran nearby, but given an effect of lightness and air by the great central shaft. Vines and ferns looping over the balcony and railing of a restaurant for employees on the top floor added to the pleasant effect of the central court.

The building had great impact in Europe, and it was also a "first" in many ways. Among the innovations claimed for it by Wright were that it was fireproof, air conditioned, and furnished throughout with steel filing cabinets, which he had designed. Other "firsts" were all-glass doors, double-glass windows, and steel furniture and seats. Wright wanted even to do the wastebaskets and telephones in his own style, but the Larkin firm had already provided for them before he had a chance to use his pencil.

The Larkin building had what Wright liked to call articulation—a jointing or segmenting, brought about by having the stairwells constructed as separate towers adjoining the building, rather than being fitted inside the whole rectangle. They served also as air intakes for the ventilating system. Wright was so determined to bring about the last-minute change of plans which provided for the articulation that he made a special train trip to Buffalo to appeal to the owners. This was characteristic of Wright, to keep his buildings "growing" right up to the end of construction—and sometimes afterwards.

While the Larkin building had its special problems growing from the many innovations, the building of Unity Temple, soon afterwards, held even more. Here Wright was working with a very limited budget, and a skeptical building committee besides. The Oak Park congregation had only $45,000 with which to build a church auditorium seating 400, plus a large adjoining room for banquets and recreation.

Even at the prices prevailing in the early 1900's, Wright knew $45,000 would not build the church in anything but concrete, so he tried to figure out how even this cheap material could be made to serve. Most of the money, he decided, would have to go for one large square room. The outside walls would be nearly identical, to save as much as possible by using the same wooden forms over and over. The custom of the day was to put a thin veneer of bricks or stone over the concrete, but there wasn't even enough money for this, so Wright decided to let some of the stones of the concrete mixture appear on the wall surfaces to give texture and variety to all those flat surfaces.

One big room—that was the idea, with a concrete slab for a roof, pierced by skylights of amber glass, so that daylight and night light would show the same effect. Instead of the traditional street entrance, with the congregation streaming in toward the minister and turning their backs on him when they left, Wright placed the main entrance from a courtyard between the big central church room and the adjoining recreation building, connected to it by the minister's study. The congregation entered along sunken foyers at each side, past the clergyman, and after the services came toward him to regain the entrance.

Wright worked all night the first night after getting the main idea, and in the next few days he made a total of thirty-four studies of the relationship of the main building to the recreation building before he was satisfied with their harmony. This was the kind of hard, concentrated work that he did not boast about to the client but that made his buildings seem so perfectly suited to their location and use.

The architect worried that the building committee would let its prejudices or misinformation interfere with the unusual design. The minister himself was troubled by the absence of the traditional New England church steeple in this flat-roofed building. Pleas of an engineer on the committee, reinforced by sight of a hastily built model of the church, turned the tide.

On dedication day for the completed church, Wright was so nervous that he would not go to the ceremonies. But by noon he began to receive telephone calls of approval. With high heart, he set out with daughter Frances for a walk, when he was interrupted by one last call—from the persistent doubter on the committee, the chronic objector who was a good enough sport to call and say that acoustics and lighting, the two things he had worried about, were fine.

But now, at age thirty-five, the struggles with clients and contractors in his first ten years as an independent architect fighting for a brand-new style of architecture had worn Wright down. He decided that after these years of day and night labor at the drafting board, he needed a vacation. In 1905 he and Catherine, together with Mr. and Mrs. Ward W. Willitts, for whom he had designed a house, sailed for a few weeks' vacation in Japan.

Even being a genius didn't prevent him from being seasick. He was miserable all the way across until the ship docked at Yokohama. He suffered equally on seven other crossings of the Pacific, showing no improvement in later voyages.

Wright was already familiar with the simplicity of line and minimum of detail in Japanese prints. Now he had a chance to study Japanese architecture—the use of light paper screens to partition rooms, the charm of wood polished and showing honestly as wood, rather than scrolled, jigsawed, and stained into something looking like embroidery. Japanese houses, he concluded, had "repose" and looked like human shelter, rather than fake castles. He came more firmly to the conception of a house as "space enclosed," rather than as walls and roof, when he returned to his drafting board.

Wright's Prairie Houses had "the countenance of principle," Mrs. Avery Coonley told the architect some years after his return from Japan. She commissioned him to design a very large house, and he reciprocated by designing dresses, table service, and linen for her. The Coonley house in Riverside, a Chicago suburb, and the magnificent house for Frederick C. Robie on Chicago's South Side, marked the high point of Wright's Prairie Style houses. Both became famous as superb examples of the best in Wright's organic architecture.

Even these, however, would probably have been eclipsed by a masterpiece ordered by Mr. and Mrs. Harold McCormick, of the farm machinery family, to be built on a commanding site on a Lake Michigan bluff north of Chicago, but it did not come off. It was a majestic concept for a whole series of connected buildings and wings. With this recognition by the McCormicks, the actual construction of the house would have been a turning point into prosperity and more commissions than Wright could possibly handle.

However, after the drawings were done, Edith Rockefeller McCormick decided that she wanted a New Yorker, rather than Midwesterner, as architect. Wright's star faltered, for personal as well as architectural reasons.

For years, relations between Wright and his no-longer-young wife had been growing more strained. He was absorbed in his plans, often working through much of the night. She was kept more than busy with the six children, and both were spending a lot of time fending off bill collectors. It was the familiar story of the too-young marriage and the later disillusionment, as each partner developed into a somewhat different person.

It was about this time, in 1909, that Wright received an attractive offer from the big German publishing house of Ernst Wasmuth, which wanted to print a collection of

drawings of his Prairie Style houses. The Wasmuth imprint
would represent enormous acclaim, Wright realized. The
McCormick disappointment, the publishing offer, and the
trouble at home, combined with the strain of overwork, had
their effect.

Wright sailed for Europe, presumably to see his drawings
through the Wasmuth presses, but with him on the boat was
Mamah (pronounced "May-mah") Borthwick Cheney, wife
of Edwin Cheney, for whom Wright had designed one of
the early Oak Park houses. After a short stay in Berlin,
Wright and Mrs. Cheney set up housekeeping in a villa on a
sunny hillside in Florence, Italy, where they lived for nearly
two years. At home, black thunderclouds of headlines in the
newspapers screamed of "scandal." The rich clients immediately turned away from him. Wright insisted that he had no
other choice in his personal life because Catherine would
not consent to a divorce. He asserted that it was more hon-
orable to live openly with Mrs. Cheney than to carry on a
secret affair, but this was certainly not society's way of
looking at things.

Wright's first "architectural life" was drawing to a close.
Scarcely forty years old, he had absorbed major building
principles and skill at matching harmonious construction
and ornament from Sullivan. In his prairie houses Wright
boldly departed from the artificial forms of fake castles, tur-
rets, and "gingerbread." In the Larkin building he pioneered
air conditioning, steel furniture, glass doors, and several
other innovations, but it remained his only major building.
In Unity Temple he had shown how concrete could be
transformed into an artistic architectural expression.

Aside from the homes, he had only two large buildings,
the Larkin and Unity Temple, to his credit. Yet he was al-

ready famous in Europe, though little known in America. And the kind of fame he was getting in his own country was not the kind that would bring clients to his door. In a few years a tragic fire and murders would apparently end his architectural career forever.

Seven

"Good Time Place"—and Tragedy

"There's nothing so timid as a million dollars!" [1] grumbled middle-aged Frank Lloyd Wright as he contemplated his Chicago office, embarrassingly free of clients.

At the age of forty-four, Wright was at the height of his powers, a striking figure with his flashing gray-blue eyes, usually twinkling with humor, and a great mass of curly brown hair, brushed straight back. But he had to use his ceaseless energy in "projects," the hopeful sketches of dream castles that had practically no chance of being built.

Wright did not talk much about it to his second son, John, who had recently come from California to run his father's architectural office, but John could see that the elder Wright was worried about finances and itching to tackle designs for the great hotels, office buildings, theaters, and mansions for the rich that he knew so well how to create.

The newspaper headline excitement over Wright's two-year sojourn in Europe with Mrs. Cheney had died down, but the memory lingered on—especially in the minds of people with a million or more to spend, and they were frightened away.

On two hundred acres of rugged slopes in the Wyoming Valley, given him by his mother, Wright had started a home for himself and Mrs. Cheney. He called it "Taliesin," for a third-century Welsh poet whose name meant "Shining Brow."

Taliesin, the jewel adorning the brow of the hill fronting the Wisconsin River Valley, was being finished, and Wright was making weekly trips to his Chicago office, to oversee the handful of private homes that were on the drafting boards or being built. Mrs. Cheney took charge of the drafting room during his trips, while she also kept up her own work of Latin translations. Money was a constant problem, and Wright also worried about his children. On his trips to Chicago he would walk at night past the lighted windows of his old home in Oak Park, to reassure himself that the children were well.

Into this picture came Edward Waller, son of the man who had sought, with the prominent planner Daniel Burnham, to get Wright to study at the Beaux Arts in Paris nearly twenty years earlier. Wright, always close to the Waller family, had especially enjoyed Christmas and other parties with them. Now young Waller suggested that Wright put his life-long love of gay musical parties into the reality of concrete and brick to bring Chicago a new experience.

Waller told him:

"Frank, in all this black old town there's no place to go but out, nor any place to come but back, that isn't bare and ugly unless it's cheap and nasty. I want to put a garden in this wilderness of smoky dens, car-tracks, and saloons. . . . I believe Chicago would appreciate a beautiful garden resort. Our people would go there, listen to good music, eat and drink. You know, an outdoor garden something like those little parks round Munich where German families go." [2]

Wright was enchanted at the prospect and promised Waller to have something ready in a few days. But he would not say just what that "something" would be like. It was to be a rush job, with working drawings in thirty days and construction to be completed just three months later.

The plans came to him almost in a flash, Wright declared later. "The thing had simply shaken itself out of my sleeve." [3]

There is no "typical" Wright building project, but perhaps Midway Gardens, the gay music and dining spot stimulated by Edward Waller just before World War I, came as close as any to having all the elements. It had an enthusiastic client with a dream but not enough money to pay for the cost. It had run-ins with labor unions. It enjoyed the close attention of Wright himself—as most of his buildings did—and it had a beautiful outcome. In the process it got modified and enriched, just as many of Wright's other buildings did during construction.

John Wright was dazzled when his father, a week after Waller's visit, seemed to produce the plans spontaneously on a plain sheet of drawing paper.

" 'Watch it come out of this clean white sheet,' " John said his father told him, recalling the exciting creation years later. "Dad began to draw. The pencil in his swift, sure hand moved rapidly, firmly, up, down, right, left, slant-wise— mostly right and left. Within an hour, there it was! Low masonry terraces enclosed by promenades, loggias, galleries, orchestra shell and winter garden popped right out of the clean white paper.

"The exact dimensions, details and ornamentation indicated by an interlocking organism of plans, elevations, sections and small perspective sketches were all on the one sheet! The entire conception as to the design which was to cover a block square was completed. He drew balloons tied to the towers like the ones we played with at home." [4]

And then, with a typical Wright gesture, the architect told his son to "fill in the details of the drawing," picked up his stick, gave it a twirl, and was off.

Had the whole scheme been transferred for the first time from Wright's tremendously fertile brain to paper in the space of an hour, before his son's astonished eyes? Wright loved the grand gesture, and surely this was one of his best. After all, Sullivan told him that he had drawn the Wainwright building plan in just three minutes. Even if Wright had not roughed out a few preliminary sketches of the block-square, complex Midway Gardens, he certainly had developed the whole idea in his head before he drew it for John.

Few people realized the energy and painstaking care that Wright brought to his work, because he did not speak of it, and scarcely any outsiders saw him during the long hours bent over his drafting board. He was much more apt to discuss the principles he felt were behind his architecture than he was to talk of the laborious hours of drawing, erasing, redrawing, and plotting scales that preceded the finished "preliminary sketch." Some of the early drawings of completed buildings, such as the Guggenheim Museum, even show considerable changes or development from the original concept. In any case, Wright was familiar with the German beer gardens and had doubtless thought many times of the "good time places," as he called them, which the world needed for its relaxation and entertainment.

Midway also showed another side of Wright's life: the constant battling with creditors and his careless handling of money. He usually carried his "folding money" loosely crumpled in any convenient pocket, which could be coat, overcoat, or vest. He even had to smooth out a bill to see what denomination it was. Much of the time there was little or no money in his pocket.

In the midst of working on the detailed drawings for the Midway, Wright looked up one morning to see the sheriff in the doorway.

"Sorry, but I've got to close up the office, lock everything up, Mr. Wright," the sheriff said, displaying a court order. "You've got an unpaid bill here for $1,500."

It was one of many unpaid bills, Wright knew, but he showed no anxiety as he courteously invited the sheriff in to look over the drafting room under the guidance of son John —for Wright had seen another person approaching behind the sheriff. In a few minutes Wright joined the law officer and John in the drafting room.

"Here you are, Sheriff," Wright beamed. "I've got the money for you," and he displayed a check for $10,000. He had just sold a batch of Japanese prints from his collection to a dealer. Then he and John went out for a glorious meal at a top restaurant, where they planned the spending of the rest of the money on various expensive items. By the end of the day, the money was all gone.

The Midway Gardens was also somewhat typical because it brought Wright repeatedly into clashes with representatives of construction unions. Wright drove himself mercilessly and expected long hours from associates like his son John. The joy of creation was so strong in him that he could not conceive why workmen would insist on limiting the **work** day or demand overtime pay for working beyond the

limit. Throughout his life Wright inveighed against construction unions, declaring that they were interested only in
power and dollars, rather than in craftsmanship. He had a
somewhat similar feeling toward contractors, who ought to
be willing to forego profits in exchange for the privilege of
working on a masterpiece, he felt. Haggling over just which
union should do which job also stirred Wright.

In the clearing of the three-acre site for Midway Gardens,
the job hit a snag when the unions insisted that only the
steelworkers union could remove a rusty old steel tower on
the property. When the unions completely shut down all
work, Wright finally gave in, and the steelworkers took
down the tower.

But Wright got his innings later, during the actual construction, when a union agent demanded repeatedly that
two artists working on the painting and sculpture portions of
the building must hold regular construction workers' union
cards.

"Yes, and that girl posing in the construction shack for
those artists—she's got to have a card and pay dues too," the
union agent insisted.

"Get out!" Wright shouted—and made it stick. The de-
mure and lissome miss who was the model for the sculpture
continued to pose, without a union card, inside the shack,
which was the constant object of attention of the male workers. She fended off the wolves by ostentatiously carrying a
copy of Ibsen's plays on her walks to and from the shack,
but Wright insisted jokingly that she could scarcely read.

Apart from their leaders, workmen themselves had nothing but admiration for Wright, however. They were likely to
flock to a construction site to try to figure out Wright's

daring use of materials, particularly wood. Most workmen, once they understood the plans relating to their own trades, were strong enthusiasts for him.

The Midway Gardens would be partly an outdoor place, Wright told Waller. He pictured roofed galleries, which he called loggias, flanking the sides of open courts. On the principal street side would be a "winter garden," closed in from the weather, with permanent masonry terraces and balconies, facing a large orchestra shell.

Wright's design stressed the horizontal lines and flat planes that he had used in his Prairie Style houses—the lines that led the eye parallel to the earth, rather than upward. Stylized, semi-abstract sculptures were cast in concrete. Although the architect had learned about acoustics in his engineering studies and in his work under Adler and Sullivan on the Chicago Auditorium, he had trouble with one of the fund raisers for the Gardens over that orchestra shell.

The man had been active in raising part of the money, so he had to be humored. Wright stuck to his basic design, but he added a couple of swinging door sides to the shell, and that satisfied the objector. On opening night the shell worked perfectly, "astonishing everyone but the architect," Wright declared later.

With a three-month construction deadline, the men worked overtime, and Wright and John often slept on a pile of shavings in a corner of the building, so as to keep in close touch with the work. Wright was immensely pleased that architecture, sculpture, and painting, for once, were all coordinated in one building to present a harmonious whole. He was always in favor of such coordination—so long as the other arts were fully aware that architecture was in charge. Indeed, he often spoke of architecture as the "Mother Art," embracing all the others. He used delicate abstractions of the human figure and the geometric forms created by triangle, circle, and T square to enhance the masonry and brick masses and to bring gaiety and color everywhere.

Creation of the Midway Gardens not only pleased Wright because of the money but also because he was especially attracted to the idea of creating a harmonious setting for entertainment and good times. When his own children were small, he was always ready to break off for a romp with them or to create gorgeous settings for parties. He used the gas-filled balloons that were his special delight again and again in later years for the big parties held at the two Taliesins, in Wisconsin and in Arizona.

Wright was counting on the balloons to add just the right note of gaiety to the opening of the Midway Gardens, but he was disappointed. Toward the end of construction, money ran out. In spite of brave promises, Waller and his associates had been able to raise only about $65,000, out of the $350,000 needed. Midway Gardens would have to get along with a lot less than had been planned.

The architect wanted to color the walls with inlaid scarlet and green reflecting glass and to put up the sky frames on the corner towers—which were also to have vines and flowers—but there was no money. Big trees to give the sense of shelter and grace to the corners had also been scheduled for planting, but these too had to be sacrificed. Even the inexpensive colored balloons, which were to have flown high in the air, tethered to the towers and jutting portions of the masonry, had to be given up because the financial well had run dry.

But in spite of all these difficulties, Midway Gardens opened to an immediate and huge success, ending the money problem right then and there. Chicagoans swarmed to the new place to listen to a first-class orchestra, to dance, to dine, to see and be seen in this lovely setting.

There was shrewd planning too on the financial front. A big bar to serve beer and liquor was placed close to the main stream of traffic in the gardens, as a deliberate temptation to the male visitors, and it did its part the year round to bring in money. The impact of the Midway Gardens' light and airy fantasy on a city which had been steeped in "realism" and solidity was so great, in fact, that Chicagoans who had enjoyed its brief life still spoke of it with loving admiration forty years after it had closed.

However, this fairyland of light, music, and good food was not destined to last long in the shape that Wright had created it. Within a few months the man who had the restaurant concession put up a big ugly sign in electric lights.

"You can't do that to this lovely building," Wright pleaded, but he no longer had control of how it would look. Soon afterwards, a brewery that had furnished part of the money did some further commercialization.

Just a few years after the garden opened, the National Prohibition Law ended legal beer and liquor sales, and prohibition—which Wright always called "The Affliction"—completed the work of destroying the Midway Gardens. Wright later derived some perverse satisfaction because the building was so solidly constructed that the contractor who tore it down went broke.

Long before the Midway Gardens were destroyed, however, Wright's personal life was in ruins. Several weeks after the Gardens had opened, John Wright was working on a ladder, painting some of the designs on the walls. His father, down for a few days from Taliesin, was eating at a table nearby and giving suggestions to John on the coloring. Suddenly he was called away to receive a terrifying telephone message: his beloved Taliesin had been destroyed by fire.

It was noon, on August 15, 1914. Wright and John rushed to the railroad station, where the only train they could catch was a slow local. From reporters pushing their faces close to his and firing questions at him, Wright got the second and greater blow. Not only had Taliesin burned, but seven persons, including Mamah Borthwick Cheney and her two young children, had been killed.

An ignorant handyman at Taliesin, a Barbados native who had become a religious fanatic, took it into his head that the Lord had commanded him to do something about the unconventional household in which he worked. What he did was to pour gasoline in the dining room and set fire to it. He locked the top half of the Dutch door leading from the room and waited beside it with an ax. Some of the seven people who died that day were killed by the fire. The others were struck down by the ax as they stooped low to flee through the bottom opening of the door or were pursued and slain nearby.

Mrs. Cheney and her two children, who had been visiting her, two workmen, an architectural apprentice student, and the gardener's son were those killed by fire or ax. The fire burned everything within half an hour. The madman who had done it was found several hours later, hiding in the steam boiler firepot, in the smoking ruins of the house. Taken to the jail at nearby Dodgeville, he died there a few days later of poison he had swallowed after the fire.

Edwin Cheney was with Wright on the train going to Taliesin, the two men brought together again by their common grief. Cheney returned to Chicago the next day with the ashes of his two young children after a moving scene on the station platform at Spring Green, where the two men clasped hands and were barely able to utter a good-by.

Wanting simplicity rather than the pomp of a formal funeral and casket, Wright had the workmen fashion a plain pine box for the woman he had loved, and he and John tenderly lifted the body of Mrs. Cheney into it. Wright had cut down the flowers from her garden and filled the box with them to overflowing. Then the coffin was placed in a plain farm wagon drawn by a sorrel team. Flowers also covered the wagon, which Wright and John drove to the cemetery, where the men of Taliesin had already dug a grave. After they had lowered the coffin, Wright asked John to leave, and he himself filled the grave.

Taliesin had burned to the ground with all that was in it. Only the blackened chimneys and the other masonry stood stark and bleak against the sky. Wright had suffered a staggering blow to his spirit. And the screaming headlines of the newspapers, over stories that recounted the tragedy in all its lurid detail, seemed to write the end to his architectural career forever.

Eight

The Floating Wonder

Slowly, very slowly, during the black year that followed the murders and the burning of Taliesin, Wright began to regain a grip on himself. He had been crushed physically as well as mentally and for a time feared that he was going blind. Day after day he stayed in a little bedroom behind the studio, which had been spared by the fire. Unable to sleep, he often ranged the hills during the night but found they merely echoed the blackness of the ruins he had left.

One bizarre note: Wright's piano had been tossed out of the window to save it from the fire. The legs had been broken, so it was propped up on blocks near the studio fireplace. Here Wright would play it, to get such solace as he could again from music, not daring to look over his shoulder at the bleak ruins outside.

In a few weeks Wright went back to his small living quarters in Chicago, but he found he could not face his children, or even his mother. The emotions were too painful, and he preferred to walk among strangers. Hundreds of letters, whipped up by the torrents of publicity over the fire and murders, collected on his doorstep, but he never knew what they contained. One day he simply bundled them all up and burned them, unread.

But within a few months after the tragedy, he ceased to
be alone. A note with verses came to the Chicago studio,
something about "roses are red, violets are blue," bringing
an unaccustomed smile to Wright's face as he showed it to
his son John. The note was rapidly followed by the woman
who wrote it—Miriam Noel, whose dark reddish-brown hair
was set off by a sealskin cape and cap. Obviously once beautiful and still distinguished looking, she had lived many
years in Paris and even wore a monocle. She had two married daughters and a son, but her own marriage had broken
up.

Though he had been separated from her for five years,
Wright's wife still refused to grant him a divorce. He was
rebuilding Taliesin as a living memorial to the memory of
Mamah Borthwick Cheney, but it was Miriam Noel who
shared it with him. Increasingly, however, she became a
woman of varied moods, leading to violent disagreements.
Her mental state and fits of depression were a foretaste of
the eventual breakdown that put her into a mental institu-
tion.

Stone by stone, Taliesin II rose from the ashes of the first
one, and Wright found it extremely difficult to lay his hands
on money to complete it, because the publicity over the fire
and murders had driven off most prospective clients. Soon
after it was at last finished, late in 1915, Wright received
some Oriental visitors, who stayed a week and changed his
life: they were members of an Imperial Japanese commission, sent out to comb the world for an architect to build a
suitable hotel in Tokyo for the merchants and distinguished
foreign visitors who were streaming through the rising, in-
dustrialized Japan. No European architect had seemed interesting to the commission, but its members heard something

of Wright in Germany. They stopped in New York, then came on to the Midwest to see Wright's Prairie Houses.

The commission liked what it saw in the great Chicago houses of Wright, with their emphasis on the horizontal line and the flat plane. These were simplicities that reminded them of their own architecture, based on eliminating all unnecessary things. The seven members, including Aisaku Hayashi, manager of an old German-designed Imperial Hotel that the Japanese wanted to replace, indicated that Wright was their choice. In a few more weeks the official invitation to design the hotel came from Japan.

Fortunately, Wright himself was already familiar with Japanese ways. About ten years earlier, in 1905, when he had made that brief visit to Japan, "in pursuit of the Japanese print," as he put it, he had fallen in love with this land of harmonies and contrasts.

The prints themselves dated from 1750 to 1785, when the Japanese first developed color printing from woodblocks. Formal art continued on its serene, artificial way. But the printmakers looked at life around them and produced, in effect, living newspapers in color. They showed the artisan at his bench, the merchant in his teahouse, street scenes, fishermen with their nets, the rough and tumble life of every day, but refined and stylized through the artist's eyes.

Though his knees and legs ached from squatting on his heels during the long dinner and tea ceremonies, Wright felt rewarded by the beauty of the occasions. He loved the Japanese custom of removing their wooden clogs and wearing a spotless white cotton foot covering, called a *tabi*. And the sight of rows of foot bottoms, the tabis still spotlessly white after walking the floors of Japanese houses, convinced him that the Japanese were indeed a cleanly people.

Wright was already familiar with the constantly recurring Japanese earthquakes, but his respect for them increased on his preliminary visit early in 1916 to study the foundation possibilities and hazards of the hotel. Rumbling earth noises, frequent shocks, drops in the earth level, and swinging motions were constantly recurring.

And always, along with the jarring and swinging and the noises, came fire, an even greater hazard. The Japanese built lightly and close to the ground, knowing the constant peril of temblors, but this very lightness added to the fire danger. The wood frames and the thin walls of paper were excellent fire materials, so hundreds, rather than dozens of buildings, would be consumed before a fire caused by an earthquake could be controlled.

Test borings showed that the land set aside for the site of the new Imperial Hotel had a crust of about eight feet of earth, but that underneath it was sixty to seventy feet of soft mud, a jelly-like mass that would quiver with every temblor. The soil was "about the consistency of cheese," Wright decided. Long pilings down through the mud to solid rock would twist and writhe in a quake, increasing the damage. Why not, instead, try "floating" the hotel on this thin crust of earth?

It was a daring idea, so unorthodox that Wright did not even feel that he could explain it fully to the Japanese sponsors of the hotel—who included the Emperor. The Emperor, in fact, was paying sixty per cent of the cost besides furnishing the land. Representatives of banking, tobacco, and shipping interests were providing the rest of the money. If they had known just what he was planning, the architect might have been sent packing.

To test out his ideas, Wright directed the workmen to dig

nine-inch holes in that thin crust of earth. Water promptly
came up in them, within two feet of the top, and Wright
concluded that if concrete were used, it would have to be
poured into the holes almost immediately after they were
dug. He got tons of pig iron and loaded the test pillars, calculating every pound of stone, metal, and furniture that
would later be piled up on top of them when the hotel was
eventually built. He even figured on the "squeeze" that
would result on that eight feet of topsoil when all the posts
were in place, and he added that in as a load bearer.
Wright's conclusion was that, when completed, the hotel
and its foundations would sink exactly five inches, which is
just what happened.

A special reason why the building would "float" on the
marshy surface was that Wright had almost immediately discarded any idea of building a high structure, with the great
beams and heavy masonry that this would involve. He
would use native stone, about as heavy as oak logs, and keep
the whole building no more than two stories high.

Back at Taliesin, Wright labored over the working
drawings, with the help of several young Japanese architects
and engineers who had returned to Taliesin with him. In a
few months Wright made the return voyage to Japan on the
Empress of China, with Miriam Noel at his side this time.
Once again, with no control over his stomach, every hour of
the long voyage was partial misery for him because of sea-
sickness. Adding to his troubles, Miriam Noel was already
beginning to show the moodiness and fits of temper that
were to embitter their life together for the next several
years.

But all was pleasure and expectation as the two stood at
the rail at dawn, where the *Empress of China* was riding at

anchor in Yokohama Bay. In the far distance was the glistening white cone of Mt. Fujiyama, the brooding presence that reminds the Japanese, with its volcanic origin, of the daily danger of temblors. Hills and mountains rose sharply from the edge of the sea, without any gentle slope. The hillsides themselves were carved into an infinity of terraces, row on row, tier on tier, by centuries of Japanese industry, to make little cultivated fields and vegetable plots. Even the tops of the mountains bore evidence of regularity—the row on row of young pine trees, put there by reforestation.

In the golden sunshine of the morning, Wright and Miriam saw great expanses of blue sea all around them, dotted in the distance by groups of white sampan sails. They looked like "white birds at rest on the blue water," [1] Wright said. In the distance, villages nestled in the hollows of valleys, some of them far up the hillsides.

As their ricksha rolled off the docks on the way to the train station for the eighteen-mile ride to Tokyo, they plunged through the midst of bustling throngs—women and children everywhere, all gaily clad, all joyous; mothers with a baby thrust into the top of their gay kimonos; men bent under great bundles and wearing the traditional blue of the toiler. Everywhere the emphasis was love and care of the very young and devotion to the elderly. Wright thought of them all as patient, respecting and loving each other, like one big family.

He was struck again, as he returned this third time to Japan, with what he considered the dominant theme of the nation—the removal from life of all that was unclean or useless. Wright called it the elimination of the insignificant, which he had first noticed more than a score of years before in his study of Japanese prints, with their sparse details. He saw it echoed again in the houses and other buildings, where all the floors were covered by *tatami*—the three-by-six-foot mats that determined the size of rooms and caused people to speak of a nine-mat or a thirty-six-mat house. Wright had been an advocate of using the machine to bring better housing in America. He was amused to find this kind of standardization in ancient Japan, through the use of uniform mats.

Wright and Miriam Noel were quartered in a suite of rooms in an annex of the old Imperial Hotel—an annex that Wright himself had designed, to take care of the overflow of guests until the new Imperial could be built. There was a small living room and fireplace, a balcony and bath. Meals were brought in from the hotel. Above the living quarters a narrow stairs led to a large studio-bedroom, where Wright set up his drawing board, with a bed nearby, so that he could work as late as he wished—and often did.

Almost immediately, the building of the Imperial ran into difficulties. No contractor could be found in Tokyo willing to risk taking on such a big job. Wright himself, therefore, had to assume entire charge, not only making the drawings, but also supervising much of the actual building and the fabrication of the materials going into the building. He would design something—and see it actually being built a few days later. During the four years of the construction, a crew of nearly six hundred men was kept constantly at work. Many were from the countryside outside the city and simply moved into the unfinished shell of the building with their families, cooking and washing and living right on the spot.

Impatiently, Wright tried to teach them Western ways of building, but the smiling, polite Japanese outwitted him at every turn. When he brought a stone planer to smooth the blocks for the walls, the workmen soon buried it under showers of chips from their more familiar hammers and stone axes. He tried derricks and hoists to get the heavy blocks up to the tops of the walls. His workmen, strong on tradition, preferred to lug them up steep inclines on their backs. He showed them how to lay bricks from the inside of the wall to abolish scaffolding, but they lashed their tapering bamboo poles together, anyway, and clung to them with toeholds. In one place Wright had his way. He got them to do without the tight-roofed shed over the whole construction, with matting hung at the sides, which was customary in Japanese building. Having won this war, he later discovered that the job would have been finished seven months sooner, and the structure better protected from rain and burning sun, if the shed had been built. The Japanese knew their damp climate better than he did.

Rather than fight the earth shocks with a rigid type of construction, Wright planned a structure that would "roll with the punch" and yield rather than resist. He built the hotel in sections, like a train, and jointed the sections together where they were longer than sixty feet. Floors were a special worry because Wright knew that with ordinary construction, where walls support the floors at their edges, a little rocking of the building tears the floors loose, and they drop. Wright decided that he would cantilever the floors— balance them in the middle, as a waiter balances a tray with his hand under the center, and this was done.

The architect also knew that in all previous earthquakes the first things to be sheared off by the rocking, grinding motions were the water pipes and electric lines, resulting in flooding the building or charging it dangerously with electricity. Rather than rigid connections, he decided to put pipes

and wires in covered trenches in the basements, away from
the foundations, and lead them up to the rooms in vertical
pipe shafts. In these shafts the pipes would hang free,
yielding and swaying as the building rocked, but not
breaking off.

The six hundred workmen and the vast amount of
building material, either manufactured on the site or
brought in from quarries, made a circus-like confusion of
noise and movement, but gradually the building began to
take shape. Wright had brought furniture from America,
which he took apart to show the Japanese craftsmen how to
fashion the tables and chairs of his own design, which were
intended for the building. He traveled to China to direct
expert rugmakers of Pekin on how to create the floor cov-
erings from outlines he designed. With a Shinto religion,
there were no Sundays to interrupt, but about every two
weeks some holiday or other would crop up, and the men
would be gone for a day or two—with another day or two to
recover.

Then, when the building was more than half finished, a
financial crisis threatened to ruin all. Wright and his superintendent, Paul Mueller, had no way of knowing how expenses were going, but there came a point when the directors discovered that another three and a half million yen
would be needed to finish.

The former directors' meetings had been pleasant social
affairs. This one was bitter. In the midst of attacks on
Wright and the whole scheme, the aged Baron Okura, beside whom Wright was sitting, suddenly leaned forward and
with a blast of language withered the opponents. His lower
lip quivered and jutted out, and he seemed as if he would
leap across the table at the others. Through the excited in-

terpreter Wright gathered that the baron told them he would himself see to the financing of the rest of the building if "this young man," indicating Wright, would continue with the work. Since Wright was then nearly fifty years old, he could not help but smile at the designation "young man," but considering that the baron was a vigorous eighty years old, it seemed like a relative statement.

This crisis was a few months in the background and the great hotel's construction was nearly finished when it met its first great quake test. It was near noon, on a warm, sunny day. Wright and a dozen workmen and junior architects were in one of the upper rooms of a completed section when a violent temblor upset tables and chairs and threw several people to the floor. The terrified Japanese, eyes bulging and faces bathed in cold sweat, rushed from the room, even knocking down and trampling over Wright as they rushed out.

As Wright lay on the floor, he could hear tremendous roaring and cracking noises, punctuated by a series of crashes, which sounded like the masonry of his cherished walls. When the swaying stopped and he finally was able to get to his feet, Wright rushed to a window, where he could see that the walls still stood. He had indeed heard the crashing of masonry, but it came from five chimneys of the old Imperial Hotel, which fell victim to the worst quake Tokyo had experienced in fifty-two years. A check of the new building showed no significant damage from the quake: no floors had fallen, no pipes or wires were broken, and a transit placed on the foundations showed no deviation at all.

One more battle remained. Wright had spent four years in building the hotel and wanted to get back to America. All of the major construction was done, but suddenly Baron Okura wanted to eliminate the big pool in the courtyard that Wright had designed as a lifesaver in case of fire. Wright pointed out that the hotel had five hundred feet of wall and window, exposed to the tinder-like buildings across the street. In case of an earthquake fire, the city's water mains would break, and there would be no protection. With 40,000 yen to be saved, the baron was firm. But Wright was firmer, and the pool stayed. The hotel opened for guests July 4, 1922.

Wright returned to America before this, but the saga of the Imperial was not yet over. On September 1, 1923, Tokyo suffered the greatest earthquake in its history, in which fires ravaged the whole city and an estimated 140,000 people lost their lives. For several days confused reports came over the cables to America, and Wright, then in Los Angeles, was told by one newspaper that the Imperial had been a victim of the quake. Confidently, Wright told the paper that if it printed the story, it would undoubtedly have to print a retraction later, so sure was he that his design had been able to tame even the greatest of quakes.

It was not until thirteen days after the quake that Wright was vindicated. Then this telegram was forwarded to him from Spring Green, where it had been sent:

"FOLLOWING WIRELESS RECEIVED FROM TOKYO TODAY HOTEL STANDS UNDAMAGED AS MONUMENT OF YOUR GENIUS HUNDREDS OF HOMELESS PROVIDED BY PERFECTLY MAINTAINED SERVICE CONGRATULATIONS SIGNED OKURA." [2]

Later details told how a bucket brigade of hotel houseboys had been formed to carry water from the reflecting pool to the menaced walls. They had wetted down the wooden frames until the fire danger was past. The hotel was one of a handful of major buildings to withstand the

quake and fire. Wright's fame was worldwide when the
news spread.

He had called it a "transition building," as so many of his
structures were, bridging old and new ways of doing things.
In the case of the Imperial, the transition was to bring Japan
from her knees to her feet, from eating and sleeping on the
floor to using a table and a bed, and thus into the Western
world of ideas and action.

For many years the Imperial Hotel was a noted stopping
place for world travelers, who appreciated the harmony of
its architecture and furnishings. In spite of World War II, it
escaped major damage from American bombing raids and
during the Occupation became a military headquarters.
Here it met a mixed reception. Americans had increased in
height in the generation since the hotel was built. Rooms
and doors designed to the scale of the architect's stature did
not always please the six-footers of the military, who were
less interested in architecture than in trying to find something "just like home."

An eight-story addition had been built nearby to accommodate the greater flow of guests.

Nine

House That Blocks Built

Back in America after the four-year ordeal of building the Imperial Hotel against the odds of a wet Tokyo climate and the difficulties of a foreign language, Wright found himself restless and unhappy.

He was now a little over fifty years old, hair brown and wavy but turning gray, his sturdy figure still lean and able to carry him through a day of conferences and work, plus half the night at the drawing board. Catherine Tobin Wright, she whose laughter had turned to frowns and care with the arrival of six children, now seemed ready to grant him a divorce. However, Wright's relationship with Miriam Noel had deteriorated. She was often moody and reproachful, but Wright felt some responsibility toward her, even while he was falling rapidly out of love with her.

What had become of the dream of turning machine production into use for the shelter of mankind? Almost a quarter of a century after his ringing declaration at Hull House, in which he had told Chicagoans that man must learn to use machine products artistically in large-scale building, he had not done much about applying the principle.

Even before he left Japan, Wright had one more fling

with romance—but this time it was with stone and mortar.
Aline Barnsdall of Los Angeles, a wealthy, sensitive woman
interested in the drama, had wanted Wright to design a
small theater for some of the experimental plays she was
interested in. Although he did sketches for the theater,
Wright soon turned at her request to designing a house on a
high Los Angeles hilltop. Miss Barnsdall had already picked
a name for it—Hollyhock House, for her favorite flower, and
she wanted the hollyhock theme carried out.

Wright preferred the name of "California Romanza" for
the house, using the musical term for a short lyric tale set to
music, but Miss Barnsdall, a firm-minded woman, ultimately
prevailed. It was something of a surprise that the house ever
got built, because Wright was in Japan when it was started
and Miss Barnsdall never seemed to be in one place. If she
was in Hollywood, he was in Japan. If he was in Wisconsin,
she would be in London, and so on. They communicated
mostly by cablegram and letter. Distance and difficulty led
to suspicion on the part of the client, and the dark warnings
of her friends did not help matters either.

When all the difficulties were over and the house was at
length finished, Wright felt that he had been sidetracked
once again from his goal of harnessing the machine to the
creation of houses. While Hollyhock House was beautiful, it
was still mostly hand-produced. Mass production of houses
was of course not new, but Wright wanted to go a long step
further and use the machine to produce materials that the
architect could transform into harmonious combinations. He
wanted the houses to be beautiful and attractive, as well as
cheap to build.

The chance to take advantage of the machine came when
Mrs. George Millard asked him to do a house in Pasadena, in

the Los Angeles area. She had been a client fifteen years earlier in the Chicago area and was one of a dozen clients who returned to Wright when they wanted another house. Most of his clients, in fact, remained fiercely loyal to him, even though they occasionally suffered, as he did himself, during the rigors of creation.

The difficulty in the Millard house actually proved to be a spur, challenging Wright to outdo himself. Mrs. Millard said she had only $10,000, and for this money she wanted a house that added up to a big living room, two big bedrooms with balconies, three bathrooms, servants' quarters, and a garage.

It was the sort of limitation that challenges the creator to do his greatest work, since all art thrives best within rules and limits. The sonnet writer must get his work done in exactly fourteen lines, no more, no less. The landscape painter must compose his picture of the village square so as to get the church steeple inside the rectangle of the canvas, and the architect must try to build within the limits of the client's money. Wright himself always seemed to do his best work when challenged by an unusual site or the special requirements of a client.

Just as in the designing of Unity Temple nearly twenty years earlier, Wright turned to concrete, but now he thought of concrete blocks, which at the time were considered a despised article, something in the architectural gutter. He was looking for some system of building construction that could be used as a basis for developing a unified system of architecture.

Wright knew that concrete blocks were cheap and could be mass-produced. They were mostly of one size and color, used for warehouses and other inexpensive jobs. Perhaps that was why they were scorned by architects. But suppose a man produced them in special shapes and did things to the surface and texture so that there would be that always-interesting play of light and shadow? He made some experiments and decided that these things could be done. He made molds in which to pour the blocks, providing some with indented geometric designs, others with strong vertical elements to emphasize columns and piers, and still others with designs that interlocked with the next block, so that the pattern crossed the block lines. Some included voids for glass.

He experimented with different sand and gravel mixtures, making some blocks dark, some light, and some in between, to give varied wall effects and tones. Even a handful of different colors and just a few different designs on the blocks could produce a great variety of patterns in a whole wall, he knew. The architect would be like a weaver, making many patterns with few materials. Wright even thought of the wall patterning as a kind of weaving.

The architect probably put as much effort into the drawing of plans and the supervising of construction of this little home as would have gone into the design of a great cathedral or a thirty-story office building, Wright noted later, with an exaggeration that was perhaps as rueful as it was playful.

Most of this outpouring of energy resulted from enthusiasm for the new kind of construction he was pioneering. Just as in the long nights of working out designs to impress Sullivan, the many hours of night toil in the little studio in Oak Park, and the vigils in the upstairs drafting room at the Imperial Hotel, Wright did not spare himself when he was in pursuit of an idea. He called the Millard house "La Miniatura," and it became, as he intended it to be, a little gem. In fact, when European architects took up the idea and adapted it to their own building, Wright declared that he was prouder of having designed the little house than if he had built St. Peter's in Rome.

Even as the walls of La Miniatura were rising, Wright took on several other houses in the Los Angeles area, using his idea of patterned blocks. He knew that the heart of the machine principle is the ability to reproduce a form or a pattern in endless numbers. By contrast, one of the strengths of architecture is variety—the ability to combine materials and design for special human uses at a particular site. The Imperial Hotel, with its cantilevered floors to foil the earthquake and sculptured walls of native stone to give a native Japanese feeling, was one example. The Romeo and Juliet windmill, an abstract engineering principle brought to life through wood and nails, was another.

Patterned blocks, of course, were nothing new. They could be cut by hand, but this was usually expensive. Architects had also long been accustomed to using terra cotta, the baked and colored clay forms, for the tops of columns as decoration, and sometimes for decorative panels and sides of buildings. Wright wanted to go one step further and put pattern into the wall material itself, rather than having the decoration pasted to the surface.

Wright thought that by combining the architect's skill at creating variety of design with the machine's ability to reproduce forms, he could at last achieve his goal of a system of construction by which architecture could make the machine a servant of variety, rather than a master of uniformity.

Although Wright returned to the theme of concrete blocks in later years, he was only partly successful in establishing the ideal. He had hoped that eventually some way would be found to permit laying up the blocks with little or no use of mortar.

While the principle of patterned blocks in the Millard house was a noteworthy advance, the house itself caused Wright plenty of anguish. There was trouble with the contractor, and a succession of lawsuits and legal claims. Mrs. Millard wanted nothing but the best in style, workmanship, and space. These all cost money—more than she had available. Wright, seeing the financial storm clouds coming, had raised some money of his own to help out on the financing of the house. What he and no one else had figured on was actual storm clouds. After the house was largely finished and while Wright and Mrs. Millard were about to arrange the shelving for her books and other objects, the worst flood in fifty years coursed down the ravine within which the house was built. It filled the lower floor and clogged all the appliances with several feet of mud.

Wright had been outspoken, as usual, in his assaults on California architecture. Now was the time for those with ruffled feathers to fire back at him, and they did. But the end was not yet. Months after Wright left to return to Wisconsin, more heavy rains descended, and this time the roof leaked. It did no good to explain that the contractor had failed to put in the metal strips, called flashings, which the architect had specified where the roof met the walls. His critics held Wright responsible for this too, just as they did for a defective culvert leading to a flood in the ravine near the Millard house.

With its mild climate and attractive scenery, California would seem to have been an ideal place for Wright to exercise his talents; yet somehow he and the people did not hit it off well. Perhaps he simply did not stay in an office in the state long enough for clients to be attracted. A former student manned the office most of the time, but this was not equivalent to the magic presence of Wright, who had his own way of bewitching clients into action.

Wright added up the total of buildings he had designed and built by 1923 and found that he had constructed 179 buildings and had designed 70 "projects"—plans that were not carried into actual construction. By the end of his life, he would claim a total of more than 700 buildings constructed, including outstanding examples in all the categories of architecture. The number of individual drawings, for completed buildings and for projects, would run to more than 8,000.

Frustrated by his reception in California, Wright turned now to "projects"—mostly because he was so troubled personally and financially. He took to covering sheets of drawing papers with ideas for filling stations or ranch houses. He designed a whole series of summer cottages and buildings for Lake Tahoe in California, including some floating cottages, but they were not built.

Students in later years would look to Wright's drawings, the projects perhaps even more than the completed works, for clues to what made him the greatest architect yet produced by America.

Wright himself thought that "the best buildings" were never built, perhaps because the combination of the realities of a suitable client and adequate financing could not be found. But what a time he had with colored pencils, and sometimes tinting, to produce drawings that were themselves works of art.

"No single approach to Wright's work will suffice; he is vast, complex, simple and subtle, and deceptive," said Arthur Drexler, in commenting on a collection of the drawings.

"Wright has written of his preference for first visualizing a building in its entirety before beginning to sketch it out. His capacity to do so may account for the compelling clarity of the drawings, but it also makes us tend to think of them as the last phase in the development of an idea. The contrary is true. Wright's drawings were very much part of the day to day process of design. . . . More than the finished drawings, the rough sketches offer to the student of Wright's work a most encouraging lesson. Masterpieces, even Wright's masterpieces, are not always born entire and perfect. The capacity to nourish inspiration with hard work was a part of his strength Wright seldom cared to communicate to the public, much less to his fellow architects." [1]

Returning to Wisconsin after the disappointing experiences in California, Wright had both a sad and happy encounter with his old master, Louis Sullivan. For twenty-five years Sullivan had been nearly without architectural commissions. Almost his only work had been five banks for small Midwestern towns, designed almost literally as "jewel boxes" —since after all, they were made to contain money.

They had parted bitterly when Sullivan, then one of the handful of top architects in the country, dismissed Wright after finding him doing houses outside of the office. Now the roles were reversed. Wright was famous for his Prairie Style houses and the Imperial Hotel. Sullivan was all but forgotten, penniless and broken in health. Wright sat with the dying man for many hours in his cheap room, heard Sullivan call him "Frank," which he had never done before—and wondered whether he himself was about to suffer Sullivan's fate.

Ten

The Darkest Years

Wright had seemed to start a "second architectural life" with the building of the Imperial Hotel, but it did not last ten years. New troubles piled around him even while he was finishing the handful of California homes that he did in the early 1920's, after completion of the Imperial. He was indignant and never forgave the American Institute of Architects when its committee to survey the Tokyo earthquake damage failed to mention that the Imperial had survived the quake with little damage.

Soon personal and financial difficulties would cut him off while the rest of the country was enjoying "Coolidge prosperity." The great depression, at its end, would hit him with especially violent force. During this period Wright was like a swimmer who has plunged far down into the water and now struggles painfully and desperately to reach the surface again. He flailed with all his strength at the elements that fought him. Always the air and sun seemed just within reach, but still he struggled, choked, and fought. It was to be a long, bleak period of reverses and blasted hopes, from the earthquake survival of the Imperial in 1923 to the "third architectural life" that began for him in the late 1930's.

A lesser man might have cracked up mentally or become

an embittered outcast. Though he was sorely tried by people and events, Wright kept what he could of his sense of humor. He tried, not always successfully, to "keep the enterprise going" by maintaining the appearance of an active architectural business. Above all, he kept hard at work on possible projects, hoping that at least one of them would turn into the reality of a commission—and a building.

Both his personal life and his architectural prospects were in constant trouble. Miriam Noel had been getting difficult to live with, but when Wright's first wife, Catherine, mother of his six children, finally agreed to a divorce, the situation did not improve. Wright promptly and melodramatically married Miriam in a midnight ceremony on a bridge over the river at Baraboo, Wisconsin. Far from helping, the marriage ceremony merely seemed to make things worse for Wright, now well past fifty years old.

His energy remained enormous, as it had to be, to fend off hordes of newspapermen, lawyers, and court officials who descended on him as his personal troubles piled up. In spite of it all, he continued to draft great creative projects, always hoping for the breakthrough that would once again find him building the structures that he felt should take their place in America.

A separation soon followed the marriage to Miriam, but that did not mean that Wright was rid of her. Miriam—and the editors of certain newspapers more interested in sensationalism than in truth and honor—combined to plague Wright with a constant succession of legal actions. It took two years for Miriam to agree to a divorce, and she drove a hard bargain when she did. She demanded that a trust fund be set up, from which she would receive regular payments— and kept right on harassing him afterwards.

By this time Wright had found a new love, a gentle, sympathetic, and cultivated woman who created for him the peaceful and happy personal life that enabled him to keep fighting off the legal and financial wolves snarling at his heels. She was Olga Iovanovna Lazovich Milanoff Hinzenberg, daughter of a Montenegrin supreme court justice. She was educated in dance, music, and literature. Some of her educational life had been spent in Russia, and she had also been a student of Gurdjieff, a man who conducted a school for "the harmonious development of man" at Fontainebleau in France. Olgivanna, as Wright soon learned to call her, was tall and striking, with masses of wavy black hair. Her voice was low and rich, tinged slightly with the accents of her native land and punctuated often with ripples of laughter when some aspects of human experience provoked her lively sense of humor. As soon as the divorce from Miriam became effective, she and Wright were married.

For more than thirty years she would remain devotedly at Wright's side, fortifying him with the kind of warm sympathy and inspiration that men of genius need if they are to keep on creating. She was a buffer from the barbs of the world, a refuge to which Wright could fly when all the world seemed to be against him. Much of his later achievement was made directly possible by the contentment and happiness that she brought to his life.

Their first years together, however, were a rugged test of endurance. "Montenegrin dancer!" the headlines screamed when Miriam's legal maneuvers brought the relationship of Wright and his future wife to public notice. The law is infinite in its opportunities for entangling a person like Wright, who disdained legal formalities and who asserted that inner honesty was better than outward observance of conventional attitudes.

Wright, the skilled user of the public statement to promote his own architectural ideas, found again that the press could be much more powerful when used to exploit his personal troubles. Miriam, given railroad fare and enough money for "legal papers" by an editor seeking a scandal story, would journey to the county courthouse near Taliesin and swear out a complaint that Wright had violated the divorce terms, was behind in his payments, or any other reason that an adroit lawyer could think up.

Serving the sheriff's papers, even though nothing came of the suit later, was sufficient excuse as a legal peg on which to hang the old story of the fire and murders at Taliesin and Wright's unconventional life. Black headlines screamed the story again and again, with all the imaginative touches that unscrupulous editors could coax from compliant reporters. It was enough to ruin any man, and more than enough to scare away prospective clients. For a time, Wright employed Lloyd Lewis, a Chicago newspaperman, in a sort of reverse public relations role. Lewis's job was supposed to be to keep Wright's name out of the papers, rather than to try to get it in. Lewis might have succeeded if his client had been anyone but Wright. The architect was simply incapable of refraining from comment when questioned by a newsman. Wright was a master of the biting phrase and the ready quip. Besides, he was by nature a fighter and saw no reason to remain silent when causes he believed in, such as himself, were attacked. Much of the publicity he received during these days also came from a habit of issuing statements defending his position. If no one asked him, he would tell his side of the story anyway.

In the midst of his legal troubles, Wright's beloved Taliesin suffered another horrible fire, which started in defective wires of a bedside telephone. Winds of a thunderstorm in the early evening whipped the flames through the roof in a dozen places. Most of the apprentices and helpers at Taliesin had gone for the evening, and Wright and two other persons fought the blaze alone at first. The living quarters wing of Taliesin was ravaged by the flames, which were advancing on the drafting rooms, where priceless architectural drawings and Japanese prints were stored. The exhausted fire fighters urged that what strength was left be diverted to saving the things inside.

"No, fight the fire. Fight. Fight I tell you. Save Taliesin or let all go!" [1] Wright shouted. Eyebrows gone and hair singed by the flames, he raced up and down the smoldering roofs, encouraging the many men who by this time had come to help. Some were lying down on the shingles, getting their breath again to continue the fight.

Suddenly, with a great peal of thunder, the storm broke, the wind switched direction, and the flames were blown backward, away from the workrooms. Deluges of rain poured down, and at least part of Taliesin was saved from the flames. Many in the silent crowds standing on the hilltop watching the battle must have seen it as the great unseen hand of Providence, moving to save the building.

In twenty minutes the ravaging fire had turned big plate-glass windows into shattered pools of glass fragments on the floor, changed the gray-green sandstone of the walls into a reddish color, and broken or twisted the Japanese statues and pottery with which Taliesin had been decorated. Coming on top of his other troubles, the fire loss might have crushed a less determined man, but Wright started almost at once to rebuild. Genius is apt to show its quality better in adversity than during success.

As Wright rummaged among the ruins, he thought to himself, "Why not incorporate these bits and fragments of pottery bronzed by the fire, these statues and colored stone, into the walls of the New Taliesin?" Creative zeal, dampened by the bitter experiences in California and with the law, was coming back. Wright plunged more deeply into debt to bring a new Taliesin back to crown the brow of the hill. But he left some grim reminders of the fire, perhaps as a warning. In the passage between workrooms and living quarters, visitors could look up through a square hole in the ceiling and see the charred underside of the roof beams. Here was where the fire had been halted. Wright left it as a constant, stern reminder of what fire had done to Taliesin— or could still do.

The rebuilding of Taliesin was one of the few bright spots in a series of reverses, but Wright was not even allowed to enjoy his rebuilt home for many months. As the debts piled up (with interest they ran to nearly $60,000 just to rebuild Taliesin, not counting his other outlays), the clients and even some friends stayed away in droves. Finally the bank took over Taliesin, and Wright and his small family—for a daughter, Iovanna, had been born to Wright and Olgivanna —were ousted from their home. Complicated legal difficulties beset them, and they became outcasts, wandering almost homeless and rootless, in California, Puerto Rico, and other places, waiting for legal matters to be straightened out.

Desperate for money, Wright went to New York and sold off some of his outstanding collection of Japanese prints, about which he had become an expert. The Japanese print, which had helped to teach him simplicity of line and openness of plan, was helping him again, this time with money, rather than ideas. During the building of the Imperial, Wright had bought some quarter of a million dollars' worth of prints for museums and wealthy friends who gave him money to do so. He became so expert, indeed, that he detected and broke up a Japanese ring forging some prints. Now his one-hundred-year-old prints were helping him to exist.

One cheering moment came in 1927 when seven of Wright's old friends and clients got together to "incorporate" him. They planned to put up money to pay off his old debts and, by means of the incorporation, keep him out of debt in the future. Their plan was that Wright would work only for the corporation and draw on it for his living expenses. He would thus be kept out of the legal entanglements that had frequently prevented him from working to his full creative capacity. How could he do any real work if he was constantly appearing in court or fighting off creditors?

Everybody thought Wright's troubles were over, but the friends were not able to raise enough money to pay off all the debts. The $57,000 they did collect was not enough to keep Wright going until new architectural commissions were in sight. A few years later, however, the idea of incorporation was indeed carried out and worked well until Wright's death.

The big projects, any one of which could have turned the tide financially, either hung fire or failed to get past the preliminary planning stage. Wright had $20,000 from Albert Johnson, head of the National Life Insurance Company, to do preliminary sketches for a giant steel and glass cantilevered office building in Chicago, but the design never got past sketches. Johnson was a friend of the mysterious "Death Valley Scotty," a man who was supposed to be kept going by a secret mine in Death Valley, California. Johnson even drove Wright across the country in an old car to visit Scotty, but the architect began to suspect that Scotty's "gold mine" was Johnson himself.

Wright's friend, Dr. Harry Chandler, had him spend a whole winter, with his drafting crew, working on plans for a big winter resort layout in the Arizona mountains northwest of Phoenix. It was 22 below zero, with a blizzard howling outside in Wisconsin, when Wright got the letter suggesting that the Taliesin group hurry down and start planning right on the spot. They were only too glad to go and promptly set up a camp of tents on wooden platforms. The stock market crash of 1929 ended the Chandler dream before it could be carried out.

Earlier, Wright had spent part of a winter and summer helping to finish the Arizona Biltmore Hotel at Phoenix. Albert McArthur, a brother of one of the promoters, had the actual architectural commission, but since the man had been for a time at Taliesin, he called in Wright to help him establish a concrete block system for building the hotel. He felt that Wright had created the system in building the California cement block houses and therefore should be the one to direct an extension of the idea.

Since he was not the architect in charge, Wright had to stay behind the scenes. The most he could do was to make suggestions and bring what pressure he could on the architect to carry out the ideas that Wright thought should prevail. It was a bitter pill for a great architect to be, in effect, working for one of his former students, made even harder to swallow when Wright's advice was often disregarded, but at least it gave him a living for nine months. The grace and charm of the building today shows Wright's genius again in a difficult situation.

A series of apartment towers called St. Mark's in the Bouwerie was designed for New York and built as a table-sized model, but here again the depression intervened to kill the project. Later, somewhat modified, St. Mark's reappeared as the taproot towers of the Price tower in Bartlesville, Oklahoma, and the Johnson Wax Co. research tower. Wright had always been a great conservator of his best ideas, and if the original client did not go through with the project, he modified the design, making it bigger or smaller, for some later client.

Honors were beginning to pile up on Wright, but they did not take the place of the cash that would have come from commissions. The Netherlands publication, Wendingen, produced a splendid volume about his works, declaring that if it had not been for Wright, there would have been no modern architecture in Holland. With the Wendingen book, Wright reflected ruefully that starting with the Wasmuth publication of his works in Germany in 1910, this made four publications in German, two in Japanese, two in French, and one in Czech—but not one full-scale report on his works published in America. Wright could run his fingers through the pages of these elegant foreign publications and savor the honors that were being heaped on him—like honorary membership in the Antwerp Royal Academy and the German Royal Academy—while he walked the streets of American cities, an architectural exile in his own land. He was honored abroad and ignored at home. An architectural magazine pointedly left him out of its list of great contemporary archi-

tects like Sullivan, Adler, and John Wellborn Root. Editor
Albert N. Marquis would not include him for years in *Who's
Who in America* because he disapproved of his private life.
Wright was getting a "worm's eye" view of society, he con-
fessed wryly.

Although no major publication of his works had taken
place in the United States, Wright still had many friends
who were convinced that he was the greatest architect
America had produced. They were outraged because he had
not been invited to take part in planning for the Chicago
"Century of Progress" world's fair, which was scheduled to
open in 1933. The plans and designs, of course, were being
done years before the scheduled opening.

Wright himself was interested—and alarmed. He feared a
repetition of "any such catastrophe to our culture as occurred in 1893." That was the time, also in Chicago, when
an emerging new architecture, tailored to America, ran
head-on into the revival of classical forms stimulated by the
Chicago World's Fair. A meeting was called at the Town
Hall in New York to protest the failure of the 1933 Chicago
Fair authorities to include Wright in the group of designers.
Knowing that if he had been employed, the dozen or so architects already at work would have been replaced by persons of his own school of thought, Wright was reluctant to
appear at the meeting, but he went nevertheless.

"Out of the top of his head," as he stood on the platform,
Wright presented three different schemes on how the fair
might be designed. Why not build a giant skyscraper half a
mile high, he suggested—one big enough to have a central
interior court in which the Empire State Building would be
able to stand without touching anything. He pictured a
building of 245 stories, rising some 2,500 feet above the lake

level, with a giant auditorium incorporated into the base jutting out into Lake Michigan. Jets of fountains would enliven
the surroundings, and lights, above and below, would bathe
the building in brilliance and color. If elevators could handle
the whole population of New York, why couldn't they do the
same for a fair, Wright reasoned.

Wright insisted later that he had gotten up to speak with
no idea of any plans, but perhaps he had given some
thought to the matter. If the fair managers didn't like a half-
mile high permanent building, how about a gigantic garden,
under a plastic canopy suspended at the edges from great
pylons? This second scheme called for a canopy five hundred feet high at the edges, near the pylons, and sloping
to one hundred and fifty feet at the center. Let the rains wash
it clean or use fountains from the pylons, he quipped. Fair-
goers would ride on moving walkways, past lagoons, fountains, and park areas, to the exhibits prepared by individuals
and companies. After the fair was over, the pylons could
stay as lakeshore light beacons, Wright suggested.

Or perhaps fair-goers would like something more roman-
tic, Wright declared. Then how about a gay and enchanting
fair floating on pontoons? He proposed a system of light-
weight cylinders of different lengths, some in metal, some of
waterproofed pulp. They would be grouped as fountains for
buildings or anchored as metal drums, supporting a roof
cover. Floating bridges and floating gardens would be connected to the buildings, and all would gently undulate with
the water movements of Lake Michigan, bathed in light
from colored glass tubing inserted among the floating cylinders. After the fair was over, some of the buildings could be
towed to lagoons and parks of the city, to be used as restaurants or good time places.

The meeting, and Wright's proposals, got some attention, but the fair officials had already made up their minds. They justified their exclusion of Wright from the designing groups by asserting that he "couldn't work with" other architects. They also said they wanted variety, rather than the stamp of one man on the fair. They achieved their goal. There was so much variety that no great or little building made any impression on the country. About the only thing remembered from the fair was fan dancer Sally Rand, whose success was based on fundamentally human structure, rather than man's design.

In the early days of the depression, architects suffered perhaps more than other professional groups, because businessmen were unwilling to risk the uncertainties of even small-scale building. What Wright got was just the crumbs from society's table. He delivered a series of four lectures at Princeton in 1930 on "The Nature of Materials," in which he emphasized the importance of letting wood, stone, and other materials appear honestly for what they were, rather than having them masquerade as some other kind of substance The Kahn lectures, to an enthusiastic group of undergraduates, brought in a little money but no offers of design.

More exciting, from Wright's point of view, was a trip to South America in October, 1930, to judge an architectural competition for a memorial to Columbus at Rio de Janeiro. Accompanied by his wife, Olgivanna Lloyd Wright, he thoroughly relished the long, lazy days at sea, but what really tickled him was the wild reception he got from the Brazilian students. His words of encouragement to them sent them stamping and shouting, and they finally hoisted him onto their shoulders.

A born rebel himself, Wright was always in sympathy

with student revolts against authority, so to the extent that he could as a foreign visitor, he encouraged the students to seek a bigger voice in their own government.

Another project, this one carried to completion, was to write the story of his life, published in 1932 as *An Autobiography*. Wright wrote endearingly and entertainingly of his days on the Wisconsin farm of his uncles in the Wyoming Valley and of his early struggles in Chicago. He told frankly about the breakup of his marriage with Catherine and of his life with Miriam Noel. He paid a moving tribute to the marriage partner of his remaining years, Olgivanna Lloyd Wright. Some people read the book eagerly for its frank disclosures of his private life. Others were fascinated by the behind-the-scenes story of the building of the Imperial Hotel and of some of the great private houses that bore Wright's name. Throughout the book rang the note of sincerity and devotion to the cause of an architecture suited to America. Wright enlarged the book, adding much more material, in 1942, and it remains a notable account of his triumphs and struggles.

Although he was undergoing six consecutive years without a single architectural commission, Wright remained cheerful and active. He showed models and drawings of his work in 1930 at the Chicago Art Institute—where he did not even recognize his former wife Catherine until she spoke to him. They chatted for a few minutes, and he learned that she had remarried.

Wright's tongue had been sharpened by adversity when he displayed models and drawings in Milwaukee at about the same time. The city had just completed a mammoth new courthouse—strictly in the classical style. Wright told reporters it would set the city back culturally by fifty years. A moment later he reconsidered and said the reporters had better make it a hundred years.

Never one to yield to an economic system that he didn't really like anyway, Wright was turning over possibilities in his mind of a new way of life. Young people liked his architecture. Why not let them help him in his work—and pay for this "schooling" at the same time?

Eleven

The Upward Climb

In the serene hills and valleys of the Taliesin setting, Wright surveyed the world and could see no reason why people should crowd themselves into big or little metropolises. From his earliest days in Chicago, Wright appeared to hate and fear cities. It seemed incredible to him that people should want to herd together, crowded into tiny apartments or jostled on busy streets. He liked the concerts and good theater that require a big city for public support, but otherwise he just wished the big cities would vanish.

The personal and financial difficulties of the late twenties had not destroyed his optimistic spirit nor his energy, even though they ended the "second architectural life" that began with the Imperial Hotel. Now he was about to launch a third "life," in which he would emphasize suburban or rural living, rather than city mansions. He would write a prescription to make the city disappear and draw a group of young people around him as a fellowship of architectural apprentices—and make them pay their own way. On the drafting board was just one moderate-sized house, but soon to come and in the offing were three buildings: a slum-area office building that would set a new mark for beauty, a low-cost house that would give hope to millions searching for better housing, and a spectacular house over a Pennsylvania mountain waterfall that would stir the imagination of the world.

The architect tried his own hand at making the city disappear with an ambitious project called Broadacre City, which was intended to show how everybody could move to a semirural situation and thus eliminate unemployment, ugliness, traffic, and farm problems. Using an acre as a unit, Wright laid out an "ideal" countryside representing four square miles, on a table top, and set up farms, small businesses, a county seat, and other decentralized activities to show variety and productiveness. He explained how his "city" would work:

"All common interests take place in a simple coordination wherein all are employed: little farms, little homes for industry, little factories, little schools, a little university going to the people mostly by way of their interest in the ground, little laboratories on their own ground for professional men." [1]

With each feature he listed, Wright emphasized the "little" and predicted that his plan "would automatically end unemployment and all its evils forever."

He envisioned great freeways with high-speed monorail transportation at the center, twelve lanes for passenger cars, three on each side for trucks, and vast storage areas underneath the levee-like structure. People would keep their portions of land only so long as they used and improved them, and the architect would have supreme power, as the county's agent, to see that everything was harmoniously built and carried out.

When the Broadacre City model—a sort of toy farm and village setup for grownups—was shown in New York and other places, the bold spirits who were already attracted to country life praised it, but the vast bulk of Americans continued their determined march away from the country and into the cities. Something like the decentralized small plots of ground for houses and subsistence farming, and small industries, has sprung up in a few suburban areas, but centralized planning and strong architectural control have been notably lacking.

Wright set up his own version of Broadacre City in 1932, when he boldly announced plans for a Taliesin Fellowship, a group of architectural apprentices who would pay him for the privilege of helping him with his work. He sent announcements to schools of architecture and other places and got a good response. He insisted that it was not a school but a chance for young people to work under direction of a master architect, practicing the arts of living aesthetically and gracefully, as well as learning architecture. Some twenty-three young people answered the first call and got an immediate baptism of work.

True, they did not do much drawing, at first. The work was in gardens, cleaning and repairing buildings, laboring in the kitchen, or waiting on table. They paid $650 a year, soon increased to $1,100, and put in long hours. To house them, Wright renovated the old Hillside School buildings, half a mile across the hills from Taliesin. For a time Wright had a whole crew of men from the neighborhood taken from the relief rolls, working to get the buildings ready. Wright paid them partly in cash but mostly in promises, under a very loose agreement. Later, when they took advantage of a technicality in the law and collected their back wages, Wright felt that they were ungrateful after he had given them jobs.

Green oak, with the sap still spurting from the boards at the sawmill, was used for the roof trusses in the big drafting room that Wright was creating next to the old Hillside Home School buildings. The trusses were so elaborate that Wright called them an "abstract forest," and his engineering calculations were so exact that when the green boards dried out, they shrank into just the space required.

Always in love with flashy cars, from the day of the old "Yellow Peril" Stoddard-Dayton in Oak Park, Wright's favorite car at this time was a magnificent Cord, a car noted for its beauty of line. Wright roved the countryside in his Cord, finding an abandoned lime kiln, which he started up again to provide lime for mortar, or discovering a patch of woods that he could convert into lumber for more building at Taliesin.

Sometimes the Cord became a packhorse, when Wright would roar off to load bags of sugar onto the fenders and fill the seats and trunk with provender for the hungry apprentices. Where to get it cheapest, and on credit, were his biggest problems, but with his persuasive manner he was usually able to do both. Etta Hocking, who had taken over the family meat market near Dodgeville, was his most loyal supplier. Feeling that Wright was doing a notable work in training young people, she gave him almost unlimited credit, running into the thousands of dollars. Her faith was rewarded when he paid her back many years later.

In 1937, the dramatic public test of the columns intended for the administration building of S. C. Johnson and Son, Inc., in Racine, Wisconsin, when Wright had piled on sixty tons of sand and scrap iron, had been an indicator to the public that something unusual was afoot. When it was completed, it would be described by sober business affairs writers in wildly poetic terms. Stenographers who knew nothing about art flocked to it as a lovely place to work. The company found that within two years it was worth several times its near-million cost, just in advertising. William N. Connolly, a Johnson advertising man, had led in persuading the Johnson firm to have Wright design the building.

The Johnson Wax Building, as it came to be known, was another landmark for Wright. Since it was to be built in the center of an unsightly industrial area, Wright knew that outside windows would give no enchanting views to the employees, so he ordered solid walls of glistening rust-colored brick. Mortar for the vertical joints was tinted the same color as the bricks, and the white horizontal mortar layers were "raked" (scraped out slightly). Thus, the rows of bricks stood out in long level lines around the building, giving the play of light and shadow that Wright always sought.

Instead of all right-angle corners, there were many graceful curves, formed by specially shaped curved bricks. Where the walls met the roof, there was no cornice or projection, but instead several bands of glass tubing, running all around the outside of the building. At night the translucent tubing between wall and roof gave the roof the effect of floating above the building, rather than being attached to it.

Visitors and top executives could drive their cars right to the steps of the front door under cover, on a driveway lined with shrubs and grass, and could park them under shelter in a giant carport. Inside the building, they entered a big room two stories high, in which the delicate columns held a luminous roof whose spaces between the column tops were filled with glass tubing. The dark discs above, alternating with the bands of glass tubing between them, produced constantly

varied patterns of daylight on the specially designed chairs and desks beneath. A balcony, with brick facing, ran all around the room, giving additional desk space.

You could take your pick of opinions about the building. Some people delighted in reporting that the glass tubing of the roof leaked—and sometimes it did, until it was cured by sufficient caulking and more glass. But the employees didn't seem to be bothered by this or by the stares of thousands of visitors. The place was so attractive to work in that the Johnson firm always had a waiting list.

"Like a beautiful naked woman bathing in a forest pool." That was the poetic description of the Johnson building given by Gus Pabst, Jr., hard-headed financial-page editor of the *Milwaukee Journal*, when he viewed the formal opening of the building. No one had ever thought to describe an office building like that before, but then, this was no ordinary office building.

"The building is so beautiful and attractive that I think I'll just put a cot in my office and live here," Herbert H. Johnson, president of the company, said jokingly to Wright. "Oh, no you won't. I'll build you a house," [2] Wright shot back, not joking at all.

And he did. The giant "Wingspread," stretching its four 150-foot-long wings like a pinwheel over the Wisconsin prairie, was Wright's answer to the housing problem that Johnson had not fully realized was afflicting him.

Johnson and the company liked what Wright was doing for them. Even before the interruption of World War II was over, they ordered a laboratory tower sixteen stories high, built on a taproot principle with each floor hung on a central stalk or core, containing elevators and utilities. A courtyard surrounding the tower, with additional offices, followed next. A few years before Wright's death, the company held a testimonial dinner for the architect and gave him a check for $20,000 in appreciation for his services, and renewed it yearly.

"Hib" Johnson not only enjoyed his house and office building but also now and then liked to tease Wright on the subject of roofs. On a national broadcast on Wright in which he participated as a Wright client, Johnson told of giving a big dinner party and being astonished when the roof started to leak right over his dinner-table chair. He rushed to the telephone to report indignantly to Wright that the roof was leaking right onto his chair. "Why don't you move your chair?" Wright responded calmly.

Even before the Johnson building got off the drawing board, with its hundreds of thousands of dollars of construction, Wright launched into a different type of adventure. He designed a moderate-cost dwelling for a young Wisconsin journalist, a home that profoundly influenced building styles for years afterward. It contained what were at that time virtually unheard of radical departures, such as radiant heating through the floor, windows grouped into whole bands, like a wall, and a central utilities stack for plumbing and heating economy. Solid walls of wood, "like homemade plywood," and a concrete mat on which the house rested were other novelties.

"Wright is known as the architect of millionaires," the journalist said to his wife as they drove past the high cornfields of mid-August on their way to a dinner at Taliesin arranged by a friend. "What can we possibly do to get an architect like that interested in such a small job?"

"Maybe we could present it as a sort of challenge," said the newsman's wife. "It's true we don't think we can lay out more than $5,000, but that's just what the country needs—a decent $5,000 house. Maybe he could be interested in designing it." (The journalist and his wife, of course, were talking of the depression years, when building costs were very low.)

On this warm August evening of 1936, the dinner was held outdoors, and the newspaperman and his wife found themselves seated on benches, at a long table. Next to them was a Welsh stonemason with a magnificent white beard. Wine, pressed from Taliesin's own grapes, was served with the meal. There was chicken, raised on the Taliesin farm, a dessert of blackberries from the riverbank, topped by cream from the Guernsey herd.

When the meal was over, Wright said smilingly, " 'Will you walk into my parlor?' said the spider to the fly," and led the way to the drafting room. There the journalist and his wife presented their challenge at last: could Mr. Wright design that $5,000 house the country needed so badly?

"Do you really want a $5,000 house?" Wright countered. "You know, most people want at least a $10,000 house for $5,000. Are you willing to do without a tile bathroom and expensive cabinet trim round the windows and doors and costly pitched roofs—the things that bring the costs way up?"

Dazzled, the young couple agreed, without really knowing what they were doing.

"A low-cost house," Wright mused, balancing a freshly sharpened pencil in his fingers. "You know, for twenty years I have been wanting to do a low-cost house, but you are the first people who ever asked me to do one. I have several ideas that I would like to put into a low-cost house, to show

America a kind of dwelling that would be much more fit to live in than the crackerboxes that fill the suburbs."

Skillfully, Wright drew out the newspaperman and his wife, learning that they liked the out-of-doors and gardening and wanted to be away from the center of the city.

"Why don't you move right out into the country and develop a small farm, with your own animals and garden and farm equipment?" Wright suggested, but they weren't ready for anything as drastic as that yet.

"You can save on a garage," Wright continued. "A car isn't a horse and doesn't need a stable, in spite of what Detroit thinks. You'll have a carport, which will be enough shelter. And you won't need a recreation room because your living room will be sturdy enough and attractive enough for all your entertaining."

Learning that they already had one child, Wright said it was more important for children to grow up in an attractive and aesthetic home atmosphere than it was for adults, because children had their whole lives before them still and could be influenced by aesthetic surroundings. "An attractive living room is the greatest modern art a family can have," he said.

"Have you ever heard of the Korean way of heating houses?" Wright then asked. They hadn't, and he explained that the economical Koreans used the floor as part of the chimney and thus extracted all the heat from the smoke that would otherwise have gone outdoors. The Koreans wound a flue in a snakelike channel just under the floor surface before leading it to an outside wall, Wright explained.

"It is a delightful form of heat," Wright declared. "After all, the feet are the part of the body that feels the cold first, and most houses are chilly and drafty at the floor level. The heated floor of the Koreans is just like a giant hot-water bottle. It keeps your feet warm but leaves the air cool around your head and the upper part of your body. You eliminate drafts, and you don't have to leave wall spaces for radiators or air vents. Would you like to be the first people in America to try this kind of heating in a home?"

The idea seemed so reasonable and Wright, a master salesman of ideas, was so persuasive that the journalist and his wife said they would be glad to experiment. Wright promised to have them out again when a sketch and perspective drawings were ready in a few weeks. When they returned a month later, he had a whole new kind of living to present to them.

"This house 'turns its back on the street,' " Wright told them as he unrolled the crackling sheets of drawing paper. "Look. We have a solid band of windows, about a foot high, between the house wall and the roof on the street side. At night the roof will even seem to float on this luminous band. In the daytime you will see the ceiling going right out, past the windows, giving the 'sense of shelter' that is one of the two great gifts of modern architecture."

"What's the other one?" the journalist asked, true to his profession of inquiry.

"The sense of space," Wright replied. "Instead of a little box of a house, with holes punched here and there in the walls for windows and the inside chopped up into little boxes of rooms, all shut off by doors and hallways, you have the feeling of space in this house. Not great space itself, of course, because this is an economical house, but the *sense* of space.

"Here's your living room, eighteen by thirty-two feet, with

one end of it opening into an alcove for a dining table, and a passageway leading past the kitchen and bathroom to the bedroom wing."

The architect pointed to the band of windows under the roof, on the street side, explaining that this would give a soft reflected light, as well as permitting the eye to follow the ceiling level out beyond the walls.

"But now look toward the other side of the living room," Wright continued. "While the house turns its back on the street, giving you privacy, it opens its arms to enclose this garden, on the other side." He pointed out the solid row of floor-to-ceiling door windows that formed one entire wall of the living room, leading out to a terrace, which was the same level as the living-room floor.

"Where does the house begin and the garden leave off?" Wright asked quizzically, indicating that the two blended so gradually into each other that one could not tell. "With these glass doors from floor to ceiling, we actually make the garden a part of the house," Wright said.

Running his pencil over the floor plan, he pointed out that the bedroom wing, at right angles to the living room, made it an island of quiet and repose, away from the noises of the living room; yet each wing could be seen from the other. Kitchen and bathroom ceilings rose higher than the main roof, and their windows above the main roof line acted as ventilators of the house, drawing off kitchen and other odors.

"The concrete floor will be easy to maintain, and since the kitchen and bedroom are all on one level, there will be no stairs to climb," Wright said.

"You'll be building the house in one operation," Wright continued. "Instead of constructing a frame and then clap-

boards on the outside and plaster inside, the boards themselves will be both frame and decoration. You won't need
anything else, inside or out."

When the newsman and his wife found a contractor and
construction actually got under way, they discovered that
they were under an intense spotlight of interest. Young
people, especially, were tired of the copying of Greek
temples and English manor houses. They were somewhat
better pleased by the rising "International Style" of severe,
straight lines and complete absence of ornament, but it
struck them as cold. Hundreds of people visited the site of
the journalist's house, trying to fathom the details of construction.

First came a huge concrete slab, riding on a bed of gravel
containing the heating pipes. This was a different picture
than the usual basement walls, half rising out of the ground.
The contractor objected to the placement of a row of bricks
at the outer edge of the concrete mat. "You want to save
money; well, here's a good place to do it," he said.

"The edging of bricks is one of the things that makes the
difference between a cheap shack and a house with dignity,"
Wright countered. "The brick edging takes this house out of
the slum class."

When the giant fireplace rose on the mat, filling nearly
one whole end of the living room, the tobacco-chewing ma-
son spat in derision. "First I put all that mortar between the
bricks, and then I have to rake some of it out," he complained. "And then the verticals, between each brick. Have
to mix color in the mortar, so it has the same red as the
brick, and then the joint won't show.

"Doesn't look so bad as you might think, though," he
reflected to the new owner. "You know"—stepping back a

bit and squinting at the wall—"those straight lines sort of parallel the ground, make it seem to fit right into the land."

When the wooden walls began rising just inside the edges of the mat, they, too, emphasized the strong horizontal lines that seemed to bind the dwelling to the ground. Each foot-wide pine board was separated by a narrow board of red-wood, so the wall, both inside and out, was a succession of sharp horizontal bands. These walls were, in fact, like a piece of plywood built up right on the spot. At the center were vertical one-inch boards of rough lumber, faced on each side by heavy building paper as a weather seal. Then, outside and inside, parallel with the ground, came the knotty pine and redwood.

The young journalist, dashing in after work at the office to see how his dream house was coming along, often encountered a score of strangers, trying to fit the scraps of wall boards together or buzzing with questions about this strange new kind of construction. They could understand the economy of having all the plumbing pipes and heating system concentrated in one central stack, but they thought "all that plate glass" for the wall of door-windows would be a terrible expense.

The new owner explained patiently that it would be "culled plate"—old department-store windows cut up to fit the new frames—and indeed he later found occasional bits of gold leaf here and there, where a name had not been thoroughly scraped away. He quoted with pride Wright's comment, "Plate glass is the glory of this kind of house," and his remark, "Think what the Greeks and Romans might have done in architecture if they had had plate glass available."

When the flat roof was on, the owner discovered that the view of the woods and distant hills from inside seemed to be so much more attractive than when he had looked at it from the vacant lot. "Yes, that's another thing architecture does," Wright explained. "It 'frames' a view, just as a frame helps a picture."

The journalist encountered a sharp contrast to his own modest dwelling when he visited the striking "Fallingwater" house in the western Pennsylvania mountains being built at about the same time for Edgar Kaufmann, a Pittsburgh department-store owner who didn't need to count pennies. Almost as soon as it was built, "Fallingwater" became the most widely pictured house in the world and has remained so. To match the broad band of rock over which the mountain stream tumbled, Wright had created great balconies, seeming to float in air, by cantilevering their supporting beams into the rock face on the other side of the house.

Polished wood tables, delicately fitted to wrap around corners; glass panels grooved so skillfully into the stone walls that now and then a bemused visitor walked right through them; great masonry boxes to hold flowers and vines that would loop over the parapets—all these bespoke superb architecture and great beauty.

When *Architectural Forum* Magazine devoted its entire issue of January, 1938, to the work of Wright, the pictures of Kaufmann's Fallingwater filled ten pages. But the Madison journalist learned later, to his satisfaction, that fully half the inquiries stirred by that issue of the magazine had concerned *his* little house.

People admired the distant and beautiful star, but what they really wanted to know about was the smaller dwelling within their own financial reach. Wright called the newspaperman's house "Usonia No. 1," taking the word Usonia from Samuel Butler's name for the United States. This was the house American democracy needed, Wright insisted. So many people asked for "something like it" that Wright designed some two-score Usonian-type houses, varying in appearance but all using the basic elements of a heated concrete mat, central utilities stack, and solid walls of three thicknesses of boards.

Within two years, the journalist noted with the pleasure of a pioneer, more than half the "modern" dwellings pictured in the architectural and home magazines seemed to be echoes, faint or strong, of his own home.

Twelve

Taliesin Accents Youth

In its first months and years, the Taliesin Fellowship had emphasized hard work and "getting the place in order." The apprentices—some fresh from college, or even high school, and some who had experience in design or construction—needed time to develop the combination of work, play, and the arts that became the Taliesin pattern. Over the years, a handful left because they didn't like kitchen duty and household chores or just couldn't stand hard work, but most of the young students enjoyed the freedom and the chance to learn by working under Wright's direction.

Taliesin was far from any big town, and there was no money, so a whole social life had to be created. After a morning's work in the garden or at the drafting board, the apprentice might steal a few minutes at noon for practicing on violin or recorder, getting ready for the weekly Sunday night concert. Boys, as well as girls, tried their hands at weaving unusual fabrics on the looms set up near the dining area.

On Saturday nights the whole group moved into the small Taliesin theater, to eat dinner and watch the showing of a foreign movie. Sunday noon they might all go off for a picnic, a favorite place being a craggy cliff that Wright named

Borglum Rocks, in honor of his friend Gutzon Borglum, who was then carving the giant stone heads at Mt. Rushmore.

The cultural high point of the week soon came to be Sunday night, when the whole Fellowship moved into the Wrights' big living room at Taliesin for dinner and a program. Everybody dressed in his best, and the occasion deliberately emphasized the contrast between the elegance of the Sunday night party and the hard work and rough clothes of the work week. To stress the formality, some apprentices served the dinner, while their mates sat around the attractive room, with small tables near them. Afterward, the Taliesin chorus might sing or a string quartet play. Often there was a distinguished guest, a noted pianist, perhaps, or a writer who would be drawn out by the architect to give his views on art and life. Sometimes Wright read aloud, laughing so hard himself at some humorous piece that he could scarcely finish. Always the emphasis for the Sunday night occasions was on music, attractive surroundings, and good manners.

A new dimension was added to Taliesin life in the mid-1930's when the entire group left Wisconsin in late fall to camp in the desert near Phoenix, Arizona, for the winter. At first everybody lived in tents on wooden platforms, fighting off tarantulas, scorpions, and occasional poisonous snakes. There was no telephone and little water. Later Wright designed elaborate stone buildings of "desert masonry," in which large colorful boulders were set into the walls so that their mass and color showed. The roofs were still canvas.

Each year the Fellowship left a little earlier in the fall and came back later in the spring, because the desert's warmth and color were so attractive. By alternating climates and localities, the Fellowship always had a new scene to look for-

ward to and a place where much of life could be lived outdoors. For a couple of years, the students all drove small red
cars in the caravan to and from the desert. The appearance
of the cars led townspeople in each place to say, "Taliesin's
back!"

In 1935, Wright was in his mid-sixties and on the eve of
starting a brisk new architectural life. Somehow, he had outwitted the economic system and was running Taliesin on
almost no money. People from the big centers like Chicago
and Milwaukee were beginning to drive out to Taliesin to
taste this unusual kind of life. Some of them even considered
the daring idea of having Wright design a house for them,
but mostly they held back because the country was still in
the grip of the great depression.

During the long, humid days of July and August sunshine,
Taliesin teemed with activity. In a typical week, apprentices
stripped to the waist might be seen swinging hoes and rakes
in the big vegetable garden, stopping now and then to show
a prospective client or visitor through the grounds—and to
listen silently to comments on architecture and Taliesin from
people who knew little about either.

The apprentices took turns at cooking the meals and
waiting on table, for both Mr. and Mrs. Wright felt that it
was as important to learn the idea of service as it was to save
on expenses. In addition to at least four hours a day of garden or housekeeping chores, each apprentice took his turn in
the drafting room, sometimes practicing lettering, sometimes
painstakingly drawing to scale the sketches or working
drawings of a plan that the master had roughed out. If
Wright was passing by a drafting board, he might stop to
note progress. The apprentice would leap to his feet and

stand respectfully at the side while Wright eased himself onto the bench and took up pencil—and eraser.

"The architect's two most important tools are: the eraser in the drafting room and the wrecking bar on the site," he would say with a smile.

A few swift lines would bring out the silhouette of a chimney mass or move a doorway to accommodate some glorifying flowerbox on a terrace. The eraser would come into play and the work of days by the apprentice be gone in a moment.

"There now!" Wright would say triumphantly. "See how we have brought in more simplicity and made the whole organic? Now go ahead and draw it up again."

Like the entertainments that usually just meant extra work for the apprentices, the drafting room ordeals could be rugged, but somehow Wright's electric energy, persuasiveness, and force kept up in them an attitude of work first and relaxation second. Part of his greatness lay in his ability to stir the enthusiasm of those about him and maintain that zeal in them for long periods—months, years, even a lifetime.

Some of the young men and women left Taliesin to carry on in the outside world the same fight with which Wright had inspired them: to make a better world through architecture. Just as Wright's recognition was long in coming, so was that of the dedicated architects who carried the message to the world.

A handful of apprentices preferred to stay at Taliesin, some of them for ten to twenty years. Jack Howe, one of the greatest draftsmen Wright ever had, turned out miles of drawings. Eugene Masselink, Wright's faithful secretary, fended off creditors as nimbly as he helped to keep the Taliesin machine running.

Sometimes this loyalty was given in spite of harsh criticism, for Wright could wield the whip of his tongue savagely when he was disappointed in a person or a job. Some clients even got a taste of the lash, but both clients and apprentices remained loyal to Wright in spite of his outbursts in defense of organic architecture.

Organic! It was a favorite word of Wright's, who used it to describe his own kind of architecture—not the fawning copies of the old styles or the uninspiring bleak boxes of the engineer-builders or the sterile and aseptic bare bones of the International stylists—but something Wright himself never seemed able to put clearly into words, except that it meant "having to do with living." Organic was like a tree, with roots and trunk growing naturally from the ground, as his own houses seemed to grow out of the ground, rather than appearing just to sit up on top of some concrete basement. Limbs branching out above, like wings surrounding the main structure of a house, open to air and sun, just as the branches mingled light and shadow and space. An organic house would "look as if it belonged there," and wall or door, wing and window, would blend into one another and with the out-of-doors, rather than look like some odd collection of shapes that merely seemed pasted together.

Visitors to Taliesin were sometimes scornful because they could see places where plaster had fallen off or a roof line was sagging. "Mr. Wright doesn't bother to keep the place up very well, does he?" they might remark provocatively to the escorting apprentice. What they did not know was that much of the time of the apprentices was spent in doing just this kind of repair work and in working on additions to Taliesin. Years and years of neglect, when Wright was fighting off creditors and lawsuits, had taken their toll of Taliesin. It would be many years before enough money came in to put most of the extensive buildings in good shape.

Meanwhile, the repair and construction work were themselves a form of teaching. "Before you design a wall in stone or specify a complicated wood construction, try doing some of this kind of work yourself," was the exhortation. Accordingly, the husky young apprentices went to the quarry two miles away and with crowbar and wedges pried out a truckload of the stones, damp and not yet hardened by exposure to the air. Then they tried the difficult job of laying up a straight vertical wall, mixing the mortar themselves, trueing up the stones with a level, and suffering the critical eye and comments of the more experienced apprentices. Weekdays, they were doing rough work—and looked it. There was seldom time or money for haircuts, so their shaggy heads and rough clothing became a familiar identification mark in the nearby villages and in Madison.

The apprentices got a new appreciation of the carpenter's skill when they built furniture and cupboards for their own rooms or learned the craft of the steamfitter, putting radiators into the big drafting room. Each apprentice thus had a turn at all kinds of construction and had a better understanding of the problems of the artisan because of it.

But it wasn't all work, either. The student assigned to dining hall duty also had the pleasure of trying his artistic hand on decorations. Off to the woods he would go, to hack off the big limbs of oak or maple to drape artistically over balconies or to make a corner of the living room seem like a bit of the outdoors. As much care went into these temporary embellishments as into the most exacting drawing, and the appreciative comments were equally prized.

Here Mrs. Wright maintained a gentle guiding hand. She found ways of drawing new members of the Fellowship into good relations with the older members, encouraging their efforts even though at first they might not look very attractive. Good posture, pleasant, respectful speech to elders, best clothes for more formal occasions—these were some of the reminders that she was constantly slipping into the consciousness of the apprentices.

The annual Taliesin wine-making, at which Mrs. Wright presided, became a festival occasion, punctuated by her own sparkling good humor and frequent explosions of infectious laughter. Using her own formulas for blending and flavoring, Mrs. Wright turned to forests and hedgerows for wild plum and grape, dandelion, chokecherry and elderberry. From the garden she took rhubarb, tame grapes, and such unlikely candidates as tomatoes, beets, and potatoes to make wine for serving later on special occasions.

Besides the bottles and crocks for wine, the cellar was practically ready for a siege, with bins of potatoes and squash, beets, carrots, and cabbage, as well as pickles and sauces, sauerkraut, cider and vinegar, all produced by the apprentices.

Apprentices had time now and then for swimming in the Wisconsin River, where a student could push a stranded log off the upper end of a sandbar and go kicking down the river with it. Seventeen miles to the south, at Dodgeville, there was an interesting county fair toward the end of summer. Apprentices pitched in occasionally to help a veterans' group festival with a portable generator. Teatime found everybody in from field and drafting room, warming at the hearth fire and consuming thick slices of homemade bread, baked from stone-ground wheat, and bites of apples, plums, and other fruit from the Taliesin orchards.

Weekends, the steady trickle of curious visitors clomping their way through the buildings turned into a flood, most of them hoping for a glimpse of the much-publicized Wright or of his wife. Taliesinites viewed the tourists with mixed feelings. The students worked manfully at the job of trying to explain organic architecture and "just what Mr. Wright was driving at" to people who had more prejudice than knowledge about building. Crowds were a nuisance, but the apprentices were also glad to see the visitors, because at fifty cents a head, this might well be the grocery money for next week's eating. It was still true that in spite of all the fame, Taliesin continued to scrabble for just enough to live on.

For his half dollar the visitor got a quick tour of the big drafting room, under the roof trusses cut from green oak that Wright called an "abstract forest." They looked at models, some of buildings already constructed, others representing projects that might some day come to life, and there were drawings on the walls. Many were beautiful colored sketches, perspectives of houses and other buildings, with the delicate shadings and greenery that Wright delighted to produce with colored pencils.

After the tour of the drafting room, the visitor sat in the charming little theater nearby. Here he saw a foreign film and munched a bit of homemade cake washed down with tea from a samovar, served elegantly on rough pottery. Usually Wright would stroll in for a few moments, giving the visitor the feeling that he was really getting his fifty cents' worth.

Taliesin was a way of life, rather than an office, a school, or something to which the student would give only partial allegiance. At Taliesin he was totally committed, in work, social life, and all other standards. Some visitors concluded that the place was a throwback to the days of a feudal society, and indeed it bore many similarities. The apprentices had to be entirely loyal to Mr. and Mrs. Wright, giving faithful service in kitchen, barn, or drafting room. They cut down the wood and brought it in by the armload for the many fireplaces. They did dishes, waited on table, took care of guests, worked with pick and shovel on the roads, as well as helped to create handsome buildings at the drawing board.

In return for this almost worshipful servitude, the master of Taliesin provided food and lodging and creature comforts for his apprentices, some of whom had growing young families. In theory, the students paid a sort of tuition of more than a thousand dollars a year for the privilege of being at Taliesin, but several who had no money were permitted to stay on anyway. In later years, some of the more experienced apprentices, who had been there several years, got small monthly stipends in addition to their living expenses.

Taliesin had its own kind of scholarships, but Wright finally came to think they were wasted. When a young fellow just out of high school would appeal to him with words like "Everyone, just everyone, says you are the world's greatest architect, and oh, Mr. Wright, I have been dreaming and praying that somehow I could get to work here in this wonderful place," Wright would occasionally melt and let the student in without demanding the usual tuition fee.

Like a person who "gets something for nothing," occasionally these scholarship holders were unappreciative or lazy. Wright tended to forget the successes, but he keenly remembered the ones who disappointed him and later declared:

"The scholarship student never works out. He is always whining and trying to get by with less than the full amount of work, and later on he never amounts to anything. It was always a mistake to let a student into the Fellowship on charity."

Celebrities were frequent visitors at Taliesin, easily drawn there by the magic of Wright's name or the chance to inspect the unusual Taliesin setup. Wealthy clients, or rich persons who might turn into clients with a little encouragement, were less frequent but even more cherished. Carl Sandburg, poet and biographer of Lincoln, came up occasionally, and Wright even persuaded him to try on the baggy pants, tied closely around the ankles, that Wright himself favored for some years. With the pants went a shirt with sleeves as wide as the trousers and buttoned at the wrist. Sandburg put on the unusual costume but didn't like it. He pretended ever afterward that he was afraid a picture of himself in the outfit might get published.

Alexander Woollcott, stage critic and radio raconteur, was a solid favorite with Wright and with the Fellowship members. His sharp wit was always tempered for Taliesin, and he ladled out superlatives in a way that endeared him to everybody, but especially to Wright. It was Woollcott who had said that if he had to reserve the word "genius" for just one man, it would have to be saved for Wright. He had demonstrated repeatedly in his theater criticism that a plump man can speak as sharply as a thin one, but in the choice atmosphere of Taliesin he relaxed and came up all smiles.

Picture him on the hilltop terrace on a morning late in

June, and one can see how the same sort of royal treatment
might equally charm a prospective client into deciding to
get this kind of enjoyable life for himself by commissioning
Wright to do a house. Before the master and his guests
assembled, an apprentice had set a low table with a cloth of
gaily colored Chinese linen, decorated with a shallow glass
platter in which anemones from the woods peeped out
against a cluster of ferns, all held up by an unusual moss-
covered stone rising from the clear water of the platter.

The sun, already high in the sky, since it is mid-June, has
burned away the morning mists from the slopes of the hills,
and the gentle breezes are wafting the scent of clover fields.
Birds are doing their delirious best, but they are also com-
peting with the lively strains of a Haydn concerto pouring
from the giant phonograph loudspeaker system that pipes
music all over the place. Wright controls the music with a
long cord, stopping a piece or changing records at the push
of a button. Haydn and the songbirds get occasional strong
competition from the white peacocks clustered on the low
roofs of nearby Taliesin buildings.

Woollcott introduces a semi-rainbow note into the landscape of greens, browns, and rust-reds with a pair of dark
blue silk pajamas and a belted coat to match, folded over his
more-than-ample figure. Large white polka dots are
sprinkled all over him. Wright is a muted foil for the Woollcott gay apparel, being dressed in raw linen, with the same
type of loose, wide-sleeved jacket and baggy pants that he
had teased Sandburg into wearing. Mrs. Wright is wearing a
big picture hat, tied with strings under her chin, which
shades her face from the glare of the sun.

Svetlana, Mrs. Wright's daughter by an earlier marriage,
appears in brightly colored slacks, with light ribbons in her

dark hair. A lively spirit who often served as intermediary between the Wrights and the Fellowship members, she was the wife of William Wesley Peters, a giant of a man who later became the chief architect in carrying forward the work of Taliesin after Wright's death. She herself and a child died tragically in 1946 when her car ran off the road into a Wisconsin River slough near Spring Green. There's no hint of future tragedy in the air today, however, as Svetlana bubbles with plans for the day's activities. Iovanna, the Wrights' daughter, an elegant young miss dressed for school, stops by for breakfast also, drawn by the Woollcott wit and charm.

Apprentices can be guests as well as servants, and three of them, including Kenneth Lockhart and Kay Schneider, have been invited to share the breakfast, so that Woollcott can get the picture of youth—and its ideas. Notables like Woollcott or prospective clients usually had the chance to explore the fresh young minds of the students, just as the apprentices got the opportunity to rub elbows and exchange ideas with persons who had been successful as businessmen or writers, or in the other arts.

At this point, in comes the apprentice whose task it is that day to wait on the Wrights' table. He carries a big old Chinese bowl of a pale green color, with a mound of fresh Taliesin strawberries nestling under a few strawberry leaves. The berries have just been picked in the garden below the hilltop terrace, and the guests make them vanish promptly, smothered in cream from the Taliesin Guernseys, whose cowbells can be heard tinkling on the distant hillside.

Next, a bowl of stone-ground Scotch oatmeal, cooked four hours in a double boiler, plus fresh eggs and baked bacon. Another Chinese platter appears, this one heaped with fresh-cut asparagus from the Taliesin garden. There is Guernsey milk in tall glasses, and comb honey from the Taliesin hives. Several kinds of jams and preserves, all made by Mrs. Wright, are ready to spread on the graham toast being manufactured by Mrs. Wright beside the steaming coffeepot on the serving table near her.

Wright, describing the scene later in a chapter added to his autobiography, declared with a touch of exaggeration that for the first three or four days of the Woollcott visit, he could scarcely get a word in edgeways because his guest talked so much. But he never ceased to marvel that Woollcott, who could be so tart in his writing and comments, was so gentle and appreciative as a guest.

This sort of breakfast, lunch, or dinner in the hilltop dining room, with Taliesin wine and candles, had a powerful effect on wealthy clients who had come to Taliesin not quite certain whether they were ready to go ahead with a Wright house. Architect Wright treated them with joking familiarity, a debt-ridden artist unawed by any excess of wealth. Perhaps because they had usually been deferred to by persons with less money, Wright's easy attitude and joshing came as a refreshing experience.

For many of the businessmen, also, it was a novel experience to be immersed for a few days in a situation where culture was king, rather than money. Outstanding young musicians from Chicago and other Midwest orchestras spent the summer at Taliesin for their board and room, just to be able to participate in this kind of communal enterprise. Skill and taste pleased eye and ear, using flowers and branches from the woods, wine from Taliesin's own grapes, and handmade furniture and decorations. True, there was no money for other kinds of art and culture, but the Taliesin group would probably have continued to "do for itself" even if more money had been available.

Was there a subtle persuasiveness, also, in the fact that the businessman at Taliesin was cut off from his usual supporting cast of secretary, clerks and typists, and a retinue of flunkies? He had to stand on his own feet and merits—and perhaps rather liked the experience.

Wright had another advantage: he had the client all to himself. No secretary or business visitor could interrupt the flow of the magic discourse. Telegrams were difficult to send. Letters had to be written by hand, not dictated to a stenographer. And that third arm of the businessman, the telephone, was practically impossible to use. The wheezing instrument on a rural line was reserved for only the most necessary business. One had to stand up to use it and turn a little crank to generate enough electricity to signal the operator. Placing long-distance calls required a special art and plenty of time. The task of hearing, after the connection was made, took extra-sensitive ears. Small wonder that the guest, cut off from his usual stimulants, soon began to relax and yield to the gentle, magical spell of Taliesin.

This does not mean that Taliesin, and the Wrights, deliberately created a maze or trap in which prospective clients were tangled. The Wrights had set up their own semifeudal barony, or estate, to have a place where the architect could function with serenity and pleasure, where the whole fabric of life would be filled with music, the joy of creation, the constant pleasure of harmonious, aesthetic surroundings. Distinguished guests came, to receive as much as they gave in the way of cultural contributions. And the prospective clients? They added to the cultural picture too, because they would not have been there in the first place unless they had a strong sense of cultural values.

Nevertheless, even Wright's enthusiastic approach to his houses did not mean that the client had to take whatever was offered. His detractors had occasionally accused Wright of "forcing" his clients to accept whatever he had dictated for them, but that was a misunderstanding of Wright's methods. He designed his houses for the individuals who would occupy them and had a rare gift of sizing up husband and wife in a few minutes, determining just what sort of persons they were. Then he designed the sort of house that he felt would best help them to live a fuller, more satisfying life. He took the sensible view that the client probably had little but prejudice and misinformation about what a house should be like. Considering the pretty terrible examples of housing in which most people lived, how could it be otherwise?

Wright, on the other hand, had studied the human scale, knew about "traffic flow" in a house so that there would be quiet islands in some areas and easy access to much-frequented spots in others. He knew about lighting, natural and artificial, and how to fit a building to its site so that it looked as if it grew there.

Actually, there was seldom any difficulty. The client did not come to Wright in the first place unless he was sympathetic with Wright's kind of buildings. Sometimes Wright himself suffered more than the client did when a building was left incomplete in some important detail or when landscaping or furnishings were ignored, changing the whole character of a house. The vast majority of clients treasured their houses and hung onto them as long as they could.

Thirteen

Creation and War

The war clouds piling up over Europe in the late 1930's left
Wright unperturbed. Although he was unsurpassed at the
drafting board, he was less gifted in his comments on world
and national affairs.

"There isn't going to be any war," Wright announced
flatly in May, 1939, when he returned to Wisconsin from a
triumphal visit to England, where he gave the Sir George
Watson lectures on architecture at London University and
later received the King George VI gold medal. His non-war
prediction was made less than four months before war broke
out.

Of course Wright did not want a war, either against Hit-
ler's Germany or any other country. He had spent nearly a
dozen bitter and tormented years after the building of the
Imperial Hotel, fighting off legal assaults, living a hand-to-
mouth existence on promises of future work that never developed, battling creditors and the indifferent public. The
commission for the administration building of S. C. Johnson
and Son, Inc., of Racine, less than three years before, had
been the turning point, starting his "third life" as an architect. Now he had a score of small, medium, and large-sized
houses under construction throughout the country.

Though nearly seventy years old, his head was full of dozens of mighty projects: a vast 2,500-room "crystal towers" hotel for Washington, a proposal for a civic center to span railroad tracks and a lakeshore drive in his boyhood home of Madison, creating seven acres of space. At his age, he could not normally expect to live through a long war and then pick up the projects that had been shelved by the war.

Neither Wright nor anyone else expected that the war would last so long—or that he himself, even before the war ended, would begin a magnificent new career in architecture. The new career, his "fourth architectural life," would see more big projects started or completed than he had done in his entire life before that. He was to bask in all sorts of honors, domestic and foreign, become a smash hit as a television personality, be able at long last to pick and choose among clients, instead of wondering where the money for the next meal was coming from.

But the picture just before the outbreak of the war was not that rosy. Neither state nor federal government, nor the much-praised private enterprise system, had any mechanism ready to help the survival of creative, artistic persons in a war situation. Wright was honored and written up in the troubled days before the war broke out, but the big jobs were still eluding him.

He was constantly embroiled in controversy, relishing the battle as any crusader must. He wrote articles on the evils of money, need for land reform, and foolishness of war, and he demanded that the sympathetic editor of the *Capital Times* of Madison, Wisconsin, print them—which the editor usually did. Reviving his boyhood interest in printing, he started the "Taliesin Square Papers," a series of tracts that turned into antiwar pamphlets.

His tongue was as sharp as ever, particularly when attacking some of his traditional targets, such as real estate
men. Wright had stated repeatedly that he believed land
should be held only by the people who were using it and
improving it. After all, this was the basic idea behind Broadacre City. Wright felt that real estate men were making
cities into nightmares by inflating land values and promoting
overcrowding. In a talk to the Chicago Real Estate Board in
1938 Wright had rattled the windows with these statements:

"If real estate were to go before some bar of judgment
where human values were uppermost, it would be taken out
and shot at sunrise as it stands. The good it has done is so
little as compared to the injustice and misery it has deliberately caused for its own profit." Warming to his work,
Wright continued:

"The skyscraper is a landlord's ruse to enable a lot area to
be sold to the people over and over again as many times as
steel can multiply it and engineers make it stand up." [1]

And Wright got his audience thoroughly alarmed when he
asserted that Moscow might well surpass Chicago in beauty
in future years.

His knowledge of Soviet architecture came firsthand in
the spring of 1937, when he went to Moscow at the invitation of the Russians as a U. S. representative at an International Architectural Congress. The entry to Russia was in-
auspicious, because Wright refused to open a roll of his
drawings at the border or show how much money he was
bringing into the country. All Mrs. Wright's fluent Russian
was needed to smooth over the incident, especially when
Wright stalked out onto the station platform and was
promptly herded back in by a soldier menacing him with a

gun. Once in Moscow, however, the Wrights were treated with the utmost consideration and respect.

On his return, Wright praised the Russians for "doing wonderful things in architecture" but declared that they were foolish to imitate American bigness in their buildings. He also got into a warm newspaper and letter argument with a Madison Communist group over his critical views of Russia and Communism.

Much in demand now as a speaker, Wright continued his bitter attacks on the prejudices that had barred him from carrying out the kind of architecture he felt was most worthy of America. People in power were the enemies. The hope lay in fresh minds.

Youth is the hope of the world, Wright insisted, but he defined youth in repeated public lectures as an attitude of mind, rather than of age. A person could have a youthful outlook at age twenty or fifty or even seventy, he declared— which happened to be just about his own age. He thought high school students had the most drive and possibility, and he was mistrustful of colleges and universities.

"Nothing has ever happened, nothing ever will happen so long as education as we know it now is in the saddle," he told a group of art teachers. "As Henry Ford said about history, so I will say about education. It's the bunk. Giving people the opportunity to be themselves is the essence of culture, for only from within themselves can they derive genuine education. Instead our system imposes upon them instructions about what to do and how to do it. As a result we are living in a near-civilization which is not on speaking terms with culture." [2]

Wright's most cheerful experience with higher education began about this time, nevertheless. One day a graying, soft-spoken man appeared at the gates of Taliesin to ask Wright to build a whole college. He was Dr. Ludd M. Spivey, president of Florida Southern College at Lakeland, Florida. Dr. Spivey's campus consisted mostly of old buildings scattered around an orange grove.

Spivey said he had no money at the moment but would pay "when I do get some," he told Wright with a smile. It was the kind of challenging bargain that Wright liked, for seldom does a single architect get a chance to create a whole harmonious complex of buildings. Usually he finds his prized building crowded in among the monuments perpetrated by rival architects.

Florida Southern was a comparatively small private college, and Dr. Spivey conceded that it was having trouble attracting students. He and Wright sketched out a twenty-year plan of building gradually a whole college campus as money became available, and this was exactly what was done. At first slowly, with students doing some of the work, the buildings took shape among the orange trees. Broad walks, under sheltering colonnaded roofs, protected the students from the hot Florida sun and frequent showers and "pulled the buildings together" in an architectural unity.

Although interrupted by the war years, building of the college structures resumed immediately after the war ended and continued through 1960. More than ten million dollars was spent on the dozen buildings. It became the largest single collection of major Wright buildings in any one locality.

Although the architect depended almost entirely on rich men for his architectural livelihood, Wright kept insisting that it was the plain people, and especially the young people, who would adopt his projects and see that they were carried out. The Monona Terrace project in his boyhood town of Madison was particularly dear to his heart.

Forgetting the principle that he set forth in a 1931 Chicago Art Institute lecture, "In architecture the job should find the man and not the man the job," [3] he appeared to offer the plan to the city, rather than wait to let the city ask him to do something. Wright drew up elaborate sketches of an enormous civic center project at the edge of Lake Monona, only a couple of blocks from the State Capitol and center of the city.

He envisioned city and county offices and courts, as well as an auditorium seating five thousand, to be built over the railroad tracks and roadway that skirted the lakeshore. The whole structure would be mostly below the city's street level, so as not to hide the view of the lake from Capitol Square. He designed the top to be landscaped as an acre of park, with grass and shrubbery, using the lake water as an added decoration in great fountains.

Sketches of the proposed building, published in the newspapers, stirred some public interest, but the city's financial giants gave it frosty looks and talked about high costs. Powerful individuals who could have swung the city to adopt the idea were still hostile to Wright because of his personal life or because they disliked his kind of architecture.

But astute politicians used the plans—and Wright—to defeat a joint city-county building that had been on the point of adoption. A dozen years later the joint building was constructed—but not from Wright's plans. His own civic center idea was later adopted by the city but ran into such strong opposition that it did not get into construction.

Although he must have realized that age rather than

youth controlled the moneybags, Wright made a special appeal to young people to fight for the civic center.

"I have a lot of confidence in the plain people, but I don't have much hope of support from 'the interests' and those who are 'sitting pretty,' " Wright said. "We can depend on young people. This is a matter for youth. And youth is not a matter of age—a person can be young at 20 or 50 or 70—it is something in the spirit that never dies." [4]

He was speaking to some six hundred supporters and interested persons in the new theater of the University of Wisconsin, which he promptly dubbed "not much of a theater." Wright said some persons had urged him before the meeting to "give 'em hell," but he added, "I don't feel like giving anybody hell. That's all past."

Nevertheless, in nearly twenty more years of comments, he gave plenty of evidence that a great many caustic barbs still remained to be hurled at what he considered suitable targets. Many were given with a twinkle of the eye and a smile that took away the sharp tone of the words, but when these sharp jabs appeared in cold print, the disarming smile and infectious laugh did not carry over. Thus Wright's reputation as an embittered old man, railing at the world that had passed him by, was maintained.

The Madison civic center was one of several spectacular projects that seemed just within reach but that lost out to the war effort. In May, 1940, Wright unveiled plans for a "Crystal City" in Washington, D. C., a cluster of twenty-one stalklike towers grouped for hotel apartments to provide 2,500 rooms. The price tag was put at $12,000,000, and construction was supposed to start in three months.

"Like throwing water in the air and seeing it shimmer in

the light," Wright said of the many-sided glass walls of the towers. And there was a touch of the old Wright arrogance and pride in his boast, "Versailles will not look like much when this is completed." [5]

But it was also in May, 1940, that the Germans began the big war push that conquered Norway, Holland, and Belgium and threatened France and England. The sharp, cold eyes of bankers and builders told them a long period of financial strain was ahead, and Wright's idea died a-borning. It was the second setback for the towers. Wright had designed the original one for St. Mark's in the Bouwerie. The tower had a "taproot" going several stories into the earth. Elevators, plumbing, and other utilities were to be carried up the central core or trunk, from which the floors of the apartments were cantilevered out like the limbs of a tree.

Although the depression killed the St. Mark's project and the war killed the Crystal City revival of the idea, Wright had the last word. He saved the idea, modified it, and turned it into the research tower added to the Johnson Wax Co. buildings in 1951. Enlarged and heightened, it became the Price tower in Bartlesville, Oklahoma, in 1956—called by Wright "the tree that escaped the crowded forest." Much more enlarged, it was designed as the "Golden Beacon," a fifty-story apartment tower for Chicago's lakefront. This flamboyant anodized golden tower was an eye-catcher, but it did not inspire any financier to back it.

When the artist goes out into the street to offer his creations, rather than waits in his studio for clients who want him enough to seek him out, he often runs the risk of seeming too much like a showman. The very wealth of Wright's creative imagination worked against him. All his life, his genius turned out brilliant projects so readily—and spread them before the public like a magic carpet, with such poetic descriptions—that some people came to think of his proposals as a sort of fireworks display. They were brilliant and amusing but not substantial.

Rising building costs and the uncertainties about the effect of World War II combined to cut down Wright's building opportunities in 1940 and 1941. Nevertheless, one bright spot appeared for a moment, when in early 1942 the Federal Works Agency asked him to design one hundred houses for warplant workers at Pittsfield, Massachusetts. Delighted, for this was the first time the federal government had asked the world-renowned architect to do anything at all, Wright rapidly produced a variation of a back-to-back "cloverleaf" type of housing that could accommodate four families at a cost of $3,500 each. This was a sensationally low price at that time for a six-room house, which would give, Wright said, "easy, dignified privacy, and unconfused comfort for two adults and as many as five children." [6]

His spirits high, Wright also proposed a portable house for government employees in thinly settled regions and a portable field hospital for the army. He declared that his war work was so heavy that he would probably have to move his thirty apprentices back from their Arizona winter quarters to Wisconsin in the middle of winter, rather than wait until May, to take care of all the extra drafting and design work.

Then came the sudden letdown. The federal agency abruptly canceled the housing project just as Wright was nearly finished with his drawings. Instead of hiring outstanding architects, as it had planned to do, the agency hearkened to a congressional suggestion that "local architects be used as far as possible" and said it was switching from permanent buildings to "demountable" homes.

Apparently unaware that Wright was used to building anywhere in the United States, the agency told Wright that it hoped he would do a permanent project "when one is authorized in the vicinity of your office." [7] Perhaps even more mortifying to Wright than cancellation of the project was the apparent evidence that the federal government didn't even know who he was.

The war not only drove away clients but also threatened to take away most of the young men from Taliesin, and here Wright ran afoul of the draft law. Before the United States formally entered the war, Wright had repeatedly attacked the American role in helping the British. He said this country was just helping to prop up the tottering British empire.

Wright's apprentices took a stand against the draft, probably strongly influenced by Wright's own frequent pronouncements, before the Pearl Harbor attack of the Japanese, against U. S. involvement in a "European war." A total of twenty-six of the thirty apprentices working under Wright's direction signed a statement saying that the draft "threatens not only to destroy us as a group but violates the deepest concerns of our individual consciences." They asked to be allowed to work as a group "for interior defense rather than be compelled to waste our lives in jail." [8]

A handful of the apprentices actually refused to respond to draft notices, insisting that they were conscientious objectors to war. They were sentenced to six-month terms in federal institutions, followed by two years of hospital service. Many of the rest, in spite of their earlier stand, eventually entered military service.

Wright himself came under fire from peppery-tempered Judge Patrick Timothy Stone of the Madison federal district court, who wanted to know whether Wright had sought to

A "solar hemicycle," the Herbert Jacobs house No. 2, Middleton, Wisconsin (1948)

Iovanna Wright (foreground) presents gifts to parents, seated far right, in fourteenth-century Italy fete at Taliesin East

Frank Lloyd Wright preaches in the Madison (Wisconsin) Unitarian church he designed

Frank Lloyd Wright relaxes in his study at Taliesin East before his 1953 birthday party

James Roy Miller

Carmie A. Thompson

Courtyard of Taliesin East (1957)

Herbert Jacobs

Some of the 150 guests at Taliesin Easter breakfast, 1959. The Wrights and their close relatives are seated at far left

Mr. and Mrs. Wright before Easter breakfast at Taliesin West, a few days before his death

Herbert Jacobs

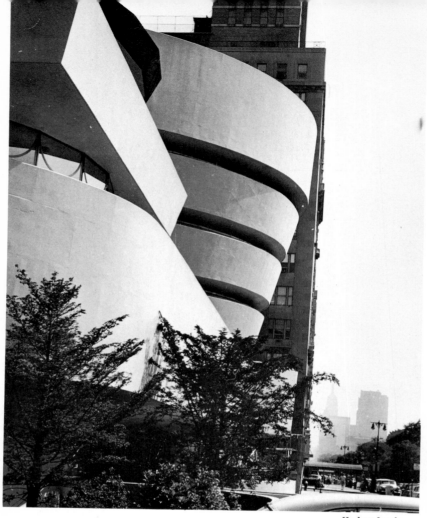

Solomon R. Guggenheim Museum juts out over Fifth Avenue, New York

With Taliesin East in the background, the Frank Lloyd Wright funeral
procession heads toward the family churchyard

Carmie A. Thompson

Wright architectural tradition continues after his death in this house of desert masonry by Taliesin Associated Architects for Donald W. Aitken, Woodside, California

influence "his boys" to avoid military service. In a bristling reply, Wright told the judge that he had not sought to oppose the draft but that the apprentices had made up their own minds on the subject without his attempting to influence them.

Taliesin subsided into an almost quiescent state. Under war restrictions, no buildings could be erected even if clients could have been found. Most of the active apprentices were gone—into uniform, or farming, or other jobs. At seventy-three, Wright was well past the retirement age for most men. Even though he himself felt no decline in his creative ability, his friends seemed to feel that the long war would retire him permanently, in spite of himself. His third "architectural life" had ended, and it looked as if there would be no additional ones.

Nevertheless, Wright continued to hold feudal sway at Taliesin. No longer scratching for grocery money as in the old days, he was cheerful and energetic. At occasional parties, guests got nips of high-class bourbon or scotch at a social hour before dinner—not because Wright especially liked whisky but because it was hard to get in wartime. True to the tradition of his early married days, he was as usual relishing the luxuries, and the necessities could take care of themselves.

The burst of creative activity had actually lasted less than ten years, from the time his domestic and financial troubles were settled until the war shouldered him away from the concrete mixer, the carpenter's hammer, and the drafting board.

But in those ten years, Wright had again powerfully affected the face of architecture. The Taliesin Fellowship in 1932 had been established as an apprenticeship training school of devoted followers, who helped him in his work and assisted in refurbishing Taliesin buildings. The Johnson Wax building set a bold new style in architecture for big industrial firms, making sheer beauty of structure an important commercial consideration. The dozens of moderate-cost Usonian type houses introduced grouping of utilities, a mat foundation instead of a basement, and simplified walls, roofs, and decoration into the housing field. The great residences, like Fallingwater in Pennsylvania, for Edgar Kaufmann, and Wingspread, for Herbert Johnson in Racine, showed what magnificence could be achieved when money was no object. The drawings and pictures in the architectural magazines, echoing so many of the features of Wright's buildings, were a silent tribute to his dominating influence.

And then there were the projects: the Monona civic center for Madison; the Pittsburgh Triangle proposal of restaurants and theater and shopping complex for a motor age; the Crystal City hotel in Washington. Although none of these was built, all fired the imagination of lovers of good architecture. They set the stage for the amazing post-war flowering, when Wright would begin his fourth and most productive "architectural life."

Fourteen

The Phoenix Rises

"I have at least ten years more (unless I get a Ford up my back or something) in which to practice the basic principles of an organic architecture," [1] Wright said in 1937. Actually, he was to enjoy more than double that span of creativity, and it turned into a true "green old age," in which he designed and built more big and little buildings than he had done in forty years. Curiously, as he moved into his eighties soon after the war years, few people thought or spoke of him as "old," though he was soon to present a world-touring exhibit of "Sixty Years of Living Architecture."

More honors from distinguished foreign societies showered down on him, and even a few domestic ones. He was respectfully and delightedly quoted in the newspapers and magazines, with his sensational past domestic life scarcely even referred to. He easily mastered the technique of being a television celebrity, when that medium came along in the 1950's, and was recognized on sight by New York cabbies and waitresses, the ultimate accolade of fame.

And how the work hummed! Taliesin suddenly found itself an architectural school recognized by the federal government under the GI Bill of Rights and had nearly sixty apprentices—double the former number. Wright at last was about to break into New York with plans for a monumental art gallery. The taproot tower of St. Mark's, conceived a quarter century earlier, would soon take actual root in varied forms in Wisconsin and Oklahoma. He conceived a unique "butterfly bridge" to span San Francisco Bay, and a marble palace for the Grand Canal of Venice—which the city fathers refused to allow.

Schools and colleges, and even some governmental agencies, were nibbling for buildings that would give architectural distinction to their localities. When things seemed to get a trifle dull, Wright whipped out the idea of a mile-high office building for the Chicago lakefront, with "atomic-powered" elevators. He sketched a "dream castle" apartment layout for Ellis Island in New York harbor, where formerly many an immigrant had seen his dreams start to come true, and he drew a "Court of the Seven Seas" as a proposed international trade center for Santa Cruz, California.

The big clients knew the war wouldn't last forever, and well before it ended they beat a path to Taliesin to enlist Wright's services. Since he was already past seventy-five, the architect may have felt there was just a touch of ghoulishness in the zeal with which certain clients who had ignored him suddenly decided to get a set of drawings while he was still alive. Whatever the client, Wright still kept his old magic touch of treating millionaires just like ordinary people. Instead of kowtowing to them, he had a breezy, bantering approach that made it immediately clear as to just who was running the show. Used to obsequious agreement from underlings or people currying favor, the wealthy clients found it refreshing to be contradicted.

The turning point toward prosperity came during the middle of the war years. Even though he had done many buildings in the few years preceding the war, they were mostly homes, and mostly small. Wright's architectural fees, usually ten per cent of the construction cost, which included design of furniture and a landscaping plan, could scarcely pay the expense of the two Taliesins, east and west. Wright even wrote one client who had been negotiating for a moderate-cost house, asking him for a $400 advance on his fees, so that he could journey to New York. Almost immediately after this, however, the shower of clients and their gold began. For the first time since he was born, Wright did not have to worry about money.

In the winter of 1943-44, Wright spent a good part of the time in Wisconsin, working on drawings. The reason was an unusual commission: to design an art gallery for New York to house the collection of abstract art assembled for the Solomon R. Guggenheim Museum. Wright was in a "circular" mood. Most of his life he had designed in right angles, with frequent variants in which he split a right angle into 30 and 60 degree angles. He had been emphasizing contrasts and stressing the qualities of materials, as in using the sheen of polished wood or the rich reds and ochres of stone or brick. In the Guggenheim he would be turning toward creation of space forms, playing with space relationships, rather than materials.

How about a different kind of gallery? Wright asked himself. One in which an elevator whisked the visitor to the top, and then he walked down a spiral ramp, looking at pictures hung against the outside wall or pausing to gaze across a great interior open space at pictures and people on the opposite side. A location on Fifth Avenue, across from Central Park and near the traditionalist Metropolitan Museum of Art, would be an eye-catching place for a spectacular building. Wright decided on a huge concrete shell, ninety feet high, made up of seven layers of spirals, each one jutting out a little farther, so that the building was wider at the top than at the bottom.

Just as steel beams and riveting had made the skyscraper possible for the magic touch of Sullivan, and large sheets of plate glass had permitted Wright to create spectacular effects in the Johnson and Kaufmann houses, so a new kind of construction, "architectural concrete," was coming into use, and Wright decided to employ it. Reinforced concrete, for pillars, walls, and floors, was nothing new, and Wright had used it in Unity Temple in Chicago. Except for warehouses, however, the walls had always been covered by some more decorative material, like a thin sheath of brick or stone. Now, under the hands of a few skilled engineering contractors, like George Cohen, it was possible to pour a wall so perfect that it did not need an artificial skin of brick or stone to look attractive.

By early spring of 1944 Wright had completed the first sketches, doing them from several points of view in color. As soon as the apprentices got back from Arizona later in the spring, he set them to work building a model of the Guggenheim Museum, hinged top to bottom on one side, so that the ramp circling the interior could be photographed. With painstaking care the model was tinted in the ivory tone that Wright desired.

"See what you can do with these!" Wright told the apprentices one day as he returned from a trip to Madison and began emptying his pockets. He poured out strings of tiny beads, little sequins, and a bag of small spaghetti rings. The spaghetti and sequins, tinted and strung on thread, made elegant vines to trail over the edges of the balconies in the model, and the colored beads gave them the highlights and sparkle that looked like flowers.

A dozen years before the Guggenheim Museum opened its doors to the public, its shape and unusual picture display methods were familiar to art lovers, architects, and others through widespread photographs of the model. Was it a well-calculated plan to saturate the world of culture with the idea that Wright's genius was going to produce a massive example of his work in New York? Very possibly Wright intended just this feeling of inevitability, because he faced a formidable opponent in Robert Moses, who had the final say on this kind of construction in the city. Moses had distinguished himself as a fiery defender of parks and freeways but had scarcely been noted as an architectural critic.

Wright bided his time, while pictures of the model became thoroughly familiar. Years later, when at last a building permit was applied for, there were volcanic rumblings in the press from the two titans, ending in a face-saving compromise. Wright made minor changes in the façade, so that Moses could claim that he had forced the world's greatest architect into conformity to the New York building code, and Wright could also say that he had made no basic changes in the structure.

Still spry at eighty-seven, he clambered around among the scaffolding during the early construction stages, followed by the respectful eyes of the workmen, who would say to each other, "That's him!" as the trim, erect figure, under its pork-pie hat, passed them.

When the building opened, a few months after Wright's death, it attracted hundreds of thousands of persons who not only paid to get in but also seemed to enjoy the special air of lightness and gaiety that characterized the building. Instead of the usual solemn museum atmosphere, the sight of other persons wandering up and down the ramps appeared to put everyone in good spirits.

As Wright had perhaps intended, the building constantly provoked controversy. Traditionalists likened the shape to a washing machine or an egg beater. Some architectural critics, among them the venerable Lewis Mumford, asserted that it was a handsome monument to Wright as an architect but no good for the display of pictures. Nevertheless, the public was indifferent to these comments and just kept right on going to the museum. Most eloquent of tributes, advertisers frequently pictured the building as background in drawings and photographs, to give the stamp of modernity to the clothes, furnishings, and other goods that they wanted the public to buy.

Meanwhile, back at the Taliesin ranches, both east and west, great changes were taking place. Numbers of eager young men, fresh from military service and anxious to catch up for the lost years, were at Taliesin as student apprentices, their tuition fees paid for by the GI Bill of Rights. In addition to the hard core of long-time apprentices and helpers, the student Fellowship became even more an international tapestry, with an occasional Italian prince, an elegantly mustached Turk or Arab, Africans, Chinese, and people wearing the brightly colored costumes of India or Malaysia.

Sunday mornings, instead of the hasty breakfasts of the weekdays, became a leisurely "dress-up" breakfast, often out of doors, at which the whole Fellowship gathered. They soon became a philosophical school hour, when Wright discoursed on his theories of architecture to the apprentices. His voice was recorded on tape and played back repeatedly after his death as a sort of guiding principle for the Taliesin architects who stayed together and carried on their work in the Wright tradition.

To visitor and apprentice alike, Wright remained the serene and dominant master of all he surveyed. A woman visitor, gorgeous in silk and sable but unaware of a new ruling on tobacco, lit a cigarette and leaned back in her chair in the living room to inhale a puff. Wright moved silently and swiftly toward her, delicately took the cigarette between his outstretched fingers, and carried it to the railing outside, where he discarded it. Though he had smoked occasionally in his later years, when Wright stopped smoking, everybody else at Taliesin had to stop too, at least in his presence.

Pepper was another Taliesin casualty. Wright simply decided that it was not good for the human system, and since he no longer wanted it for himself, he saw no reason why it should be offered to anyone else. It wasn't. There were a rugged few months also, in the early 1940's, when Wright decided that two meals a day were enough for anybody. Though many of them were doing hard outdoor labor, the apprentices had to go along with this idea until the rule changed.

Wright, in spite of his own dominance and prosperity, still had little use for the works of his fellow architects—and frequently said so. On one occasion he addressed a group of Indiana architects with the words, "Gentlemen, you are withering on the vine." [2] He himself had never joined any association of architects, state or national, though many such foreign groups had conferred honorary memberships on him.

He was touched—but not to the point of losing his head— when the American Institute of Architects awarded him its gold medal, highest honor of the society, in 1949. He had spoken so often, and so disparagingly, of his fellow architects that a rasping minority of the membership protested the award.

Just before the day of the ceremony came, Wright telegraphed the architectural journals the following handsome statement:

"When a professional society dignifies itself by awarding the highest honor within its gift regardless of affiliation, bias or rebellion, it shames non co-operation. My hat is off to the A.I.A." [3]

When the actual medal was given to him in ceremonies in Houston, Texas, on March 17, 1949, he was viewing it with a trifle more perspective. He said:

"It's been a long time coming—but here it is—and I'm extremely grateful. I don't think it is going to have any effect on my future." This was a double-barreled reference, both to the fact that Wright was on the eve of his eightieth birthday anniversary and that he had no intention of changing his own style of architecture. In this euphoric atmosphere of good feeling, the leaders of the A.I.A. clustered around him, and one of them said, rather wistfully, "Of course, you'll join us now, won't you, Frank?"

"No, of course not," [4] Wright shot back at him—and forgot to pick up his medal when he walked off the platform, but retrieved it later.

The A.I.A. medal came just thirty years after his first honor, given to him in 1919 in Japan. After that, the honorary degrees, awards, medals, and memberships in learned societies almost needed a separate catalogue.

The old fire and sharp tongue were still there to describe architecture that he did not like, which included most of the work of his contemporaries—but he was mellowing with success and praise.

He bewildered a young University of Wisconsin student who asked him, near his seventy-ninth birthday, "What do you consider your greatest achievement?"

Wright replied: "The fact that I'm alive and kicking to-day." [5]

Calling architecture "the blind spot of our civilization," he gave this advice to London architectural students when he was asked to hand out prizes to them in 1950:

"No one knows anything about architecture. For 500 years the thing has been going downhill until no one knows a good building from a bad one.

"I hope you realize prizes mean nothing. Judges throw out the best and the worst, and prizes as a result of competition go to the average of the average of the averages." [6]

There spoke the man who had always refused to enter architectural competitions and who was convinced that only the individual artist, not "teamwork," could produce a real work of art.

As the narrow upright slab of the United Nations Secretariat building began rising in New York, Wright quoted a real estate broker who said "the slab's the thing" and commented:

"Well, every graveyard, if it could, would say amen to that. . . . The Slab is now truly epitaph in New York City." [7]

Sometimes he could be both sharp and kind in the same sentence, as when he visited San Francisco and said:

"San Francisco is the only city I can think of that can survive all the things you people are doing to it and still look beautiful." [8]

When the National Institute of Arts and Letters awarded Wright its gold medal in 1953, he failed to deliver the cus-

tomary blast at current architecture, but instead declared
mildly:

"A shadow falls: I feel coming on me a strange disease—
humility." [9]

Even the University of Wisconsin, which he had attended
for about a year and a half in 1886-87, conferred an honorary degree on him during his eighty-seventh year. There was
still considerable faculty opposition to the idea, which indi-
cates the extent to which Wright's acts and statements had
stirred people in his native state.

Church leaders, who had been noticeably absent during
the era of Wright's domestic difficulties, were now joining
the chorus of praise of Wright and even giving him the more
tangible honor of commissions. In the rapid surge of church
construction following the end of World War II, Wright had
his own chance to do something unorthodox. The First Unitarian Society of Madison, of which he had been a lifelong
member, was selling its valuable downtown site and asked
Wright to do a new building on the outskirts of town.
Wright designed an enormous glass "prow" at the front,
sheltered under an upward-sloping roof of copper.

Did he also perpetrate an architectural pun? Some Uni-
tarians, whose theme is the oneness of man and nature, as
shown by their Unitarian name, thought the architect used a
building pattern reminiscent of the Trinity. The auditorium
and each of the major rooms was in the form of a triangle, as
were the columns. The cement floor was scored in diamond-
shaped double triangles. If he did have any such thoughts,
he never publicly expressed them and declared solemnly
that the shape of the building, and especially the roof, was
inspired by the idea of hands held together in prayer.

The small congregation (one member later described the

vote for Wright for architect as "like a moth attracted to the flame") had hauled stone and done similar rough work. The women wove a gaily patterned curtain in an intricate design on looms brought in for them from Taliesin, which was used to close off the hearth room from the auditorium. But the members just didn't have enough money or energy left to finish the building. The congregation endured makeshift partitions, cheesecloth for some windows, and "funeral parlor" chairs to sit on. To Wright, the building was an eyesore in that condition, and he determined to do something about it.

He sent most of his crew of Taliesin apprentices to the church to work for a month. They built pews, plastered the ceiling, constructed door and window frames. His own bulldozer, piloted enthusiastically by his son-in-law, William Wesley Peters, graded the land around the building. Wright ordered great hangings of gold-colored cloth for the windows at the prow and astonished the contractor by ordering him to remove extra braces that the man had put in the glass of the prow.

"But, Mr. Wright, the glass will collapse!" the contractor pleaded.

"Take out those braces!" Wright repeated.

The contractor, moving gingerly, removed the braces— and nothing at all happened to the glass.

At one point, some casual visitors to the church were amazed when they noted a recumbent figure stretched out on one of the pews, porkpie hat and Malacca cane at his side, snoozing gently under a topcoat. It was Wright, taking his regular afternoon nap, amid the din of saws and hammers, which was the kind of lullaby he enjoyed as much as Brahms or Beethoven.

The church was so unusual that a committee chairman sent a series of questions to Wright, puzzled to know how the building would function.

"Why the big overhangs at the prow, and why are the overhangs in other places so close to the ground?" the chairman asked.

"Why are your ears so large—?" Wright responded quizzically. "Or why does your hat brim stay so close to your eyes?"

"Why are the windows designed so that the children cannot see out of them in the Sunday School room?" the questioner persisted.

"Children are there to pay attention to their teachers," Wright replied. "But sunlight is good for them. So they have it. The little beggars do not appreciate landscape even if there was one. There is none there, so the teacher has a chance." [10]

In response to a question on why there were windows for the congregation to look out of during the service, Wright suggested this might be a pleasant contrast from looking too long at the preacher.

To help finances of the church, Wright gave two lectures there, but in typical Taliesin style, the preparations ran right down to the last minute. An hour before the audience was to arrive, a truck drove up with a big piece of plate glass for an important opening. Wright, about to leave to change to his more formal clothes, commandeered the truck driver and a newspaper reporter to set the heavy glass in place, and himself nailed a couple of cleats to hold it.

At that moment a long, narrow roll of carpeting also arrived, and once more Wright commandeered the reporter. As the carpeting was placed in exact position and unrolled,

Wright gave a thankful sigh and declared, "Now, *there's* your church!"

And to emphasize that religion, as well as the rest of life, should be experienced in beautiful surroundings, Wright had his secretary inscribe this old Oriental motto in gold leaf letters across the whole width of the balcony:

"Do you have a loaf of bread break the loaf in two and give the half of it for some flowers of the narcissus, for the bread feeds the body indeed but the flowers feed the soul."

□ Fifteen

The Golden Shower

"My first million-dollar fee!" Wright chortled to friends when he got the commission to design the Rogers-Lacy Hotel for Dallas, Texas. The work came to him near the close of World War II. He sketched a big square building, with a soaring tower beside it for extra rooms, and promptly started on working drawings. Again, however, there was a slip-up, and the hotel did not move toward construction. Since his fee would have been based in part on supervision during construction, the million dollar report was perhaps premature.

The Dallas hotel, however, was a symbol of new times. Wright also told friends that henceforth he would speak only twelve times a year, just once a month, and would demand a fee of a thousand dollars for each talk. Scarcely eight years earlier he had talked often without a fee, or for as little as ten dollars. He spoke all over the nation, and front page pictures made the nation familiar with his cape, flowing tie, mass of white hair, and low-crowned hat. "It has an overhang, like my houses. It's a hat that has a sense of shelter," [1] Wright explained smilingly. Everywhere he announced spectacular new projects or goaded cities with instant airport comments blasting their cherished new buildings.

A born lover of audiences, and now a sort of national folk-hero, Wright of course did not stick to his limit of one speech a month. He spoke always without notes, in an informal, chatty manner. He liked black, which set off his mass of white hair, and often he would have one of his gold medals hanging on a ribbon from his neck. He would absent-mindedly play with the medal while talking. The speeches were pretty much the same: attacking most college education as a waste of time, praising high school students as best fitted for the kind of training he favored, and lashing out at whatever brand of architecture happened to be sheltering him and the audience at the moment.

Wright set the imagination of the country afire in 1949 when he suggested that a man could build his own house out of cement blocks for a little as $1,500. He proposed rectangles of concrete about three feet long and a foot and a half wide. They were actually frames, with a thin skin of concrete inside the frame. The blocks would be grooved at the edges to hold steel rods for strengthening walls. Wright said a man could make wooden forms and pour his own blocks, perhaps in several sizes and patterns. Then, with the rods in the ends of the blocks, he would lay up his own walls, putting in a little mortar mix to hold them together.

A bathroom ready packaged from some big supply house, with the homeowner merely connecting two or three pipes to the water system, was another proposal by Wright. This type of factory-assembled bathroom had been a dream of many a builder, but it ran up against the practicalities of labor unions and local suppliers. They not only wanted no part of it, but also would see to it that no other sections of the house would get built if the prefab bathroom were installed.

Though it drew many letters and visits to Taliesin from eager prospective homeowners, the do-it-yourself concrete block house Wright envisioned produced only a couple of finished dwellings, and there was no visible mass movement to adopt it. Wright explained the general process in his book, *The Natural House,* but he never found the time available or the right client to work out satisfactory and easy details of doing it.

Though his designs for moderate-cost houses had powerfully influenced all building, Wright realized that he had remained the architect of those in upper income levels. Nevertheless, he knew that style and quality are never cheap.

"There is no low-cost housing problem," he said once. "It's only a problem of people who want to get too much too cheaply." [2]

Wright also tried his hand at a prefabricated house, using plain concrete blocks for the central portion, but only a few were built. He talked often of "building for democracy," but he remained essentially the nonconformist, designing highly individual houses for specific persons. Neither the "prefab" nor concrete block houses drew his full attention. Yet even a prefab or a concrete block house carried the stamp of his individuality. A New York writer, looking at Wright's first prefab in that area, was still impressed by the way in which the architect had marked it as his own. She wrote:

"Mr. Wright is, perhaps, the true owner of every house he ever designed; his clients merely borrow it to live in. He was finicky down to the last details of the furnishings." [3]

Any client, from the earliest to the last, would have echoed these sentiments. On the other hand, few of them would have begrudged his presence. They knew that it was just this attention to detail, the insistence on absolute completion, that made the difference between a work of art and a misfit.

Perhaps Wright was having too much fun enjoying the sensation of wealth, and the public acclaim that was coming his way more and more, to be concerned with prefabs. Some very old bills, dating back a score of years or more, got paid off during these days. Taliesin, which had been a sort of construction practice ground for generations of student apprentices, suddenly had its face lifted. Hired workmen came in to repair roofs and walls, as well as to alter and remodel many of the buildings. Visitors who had grown used to cracked stucco and sagging doors were astonished to find almost overnight a resplendent Taliesin, all plastered and painted.

Wright chuckled broadly, though he was irritated at first, when a San Francisco undertaker called him up after midnight one night. "I've got the most beautiful lot in San Francisco, and I want the world's greatest architect to design a mortuary for it," [4] the man told Wright.

As Wright dug into the details of the funeral business, he became fascinated, but he conceded: "I would come back home now and then wondering if I felt as well as I should." [5] What kept up his spirits, strangely, was memory of the comment of the undertaker, who always referred to the deceased persons of his trade as "the merchandise." The description tickled Wright's fancy. He laid out a group of five chapels and designed a special entrance for the arrival of "the merchandise," but the structure was not built.

Though most architects scorn "remodeling jobs," Wright even took a fling at this, also in San Francisco, when he altered the interior of an old warehouse into something like the Guggenheim Museum—a curved ramp going around the central room, with merchandise and art objects on display along the walls, under a lighted roof, which seemed to be made of floating bubbles. He created a windowless front of buff-colored bricks, with a simple Roman arch entry at one side, leading the eye into the store. As the V. C. Morris store, in Maiden Lane, it attracted many sight-seers, who came to see the building and stayed to buy. It was another example, like the Johnson Wax building, of good architecture acting as salesman.

Another San Francisco project at about this time was for a new bridge to span the bay. Wright called it a "butterfly type" bridge, because it was made up of a succession of cantilevered wings jutting out from each side of a big central pillar. The bridge was formed as each pair of wings touched. He said it would be economical up to spans of two hundred feet between supports. Wright offered the same type of bridge to span the Wisconsin River near his home at Taliesin, but the Wisconsin Highway Commission decided, predictably, on a high-truss steel bridge. When a truck smacked a corner of the truss, putting the bridge out of commission for several weeks, Wright thought it served the highway department just right.

"Our highway commission is committed to the high-truss steel bridge," Wright snorted. "The bureaucracy it represents has therefore committed the state to the old-fashioned contraption which belongs back in pioneering days with the public service corporations' poles and wires. Both are an outrage upon the landscape and an insult to the culture of the state." [6]

To prove that he meant what he said about utility poles,

Wright at his own expense caused telephone and electric wires near Taliesin to be put under ground. It was an expensive gesture, but it carried out Wright's principle of dedication to beauty.

Droves of prospective clients were wheeling the roads to Taliesin, but now Wright could pick and choose among them. He liked the challenges of unusual or spectacular sites, like the many-windowed house perched on a cliff at the edge of the Pacific. Another was a complex of houses for the owner and his plantation workers to be built next to a cypress swamp.

Frequently, a really big project was tantalizingly almost within reach, but it always slipped away. One of these was a mammoth design for a sports club and resort in a Hollywood canyon owned by Huntington Hartford. Wright lavished all his care, and dozens of colored pencils, on a panoramic sketch, but the project stayed just a project. A group of Pittsburgh industrialists gave him $25,000 to "play around" with ideas on how to revive the Golden Triangle at the heart of the city, which had become a slum area. Wright responded with a several-story motor age community center, in which people could drive their cars on all the ramp levels, getting service at stores, restaurants, and practically everywhere else except at unsuited places like the theater in the building. He threw in two suspension bridges for good measure, but the Pittsburgh industrialists wanted tall buildings, and eventually got them.

Although there were many projects for private houses that stayed merely ideas, there were also a surprising number that got built. During the three years of 1950, 1951, and 1952, for instance, there were at least forty private homes built, of which twenty-five were completed in 1951.

Wright was now well into his eighties, but he still showed the enormous drive of creative energy that is one of the marks of genius.

The chance for the United States government to commission Wright to do the new U. S. Air Force Academy near Colorado Springs would have given him an opportunity to show what he could do with a really gigantic project, but he did not get the commission. In fact, leaders of veterans' organizations threatened to "expose" him as a person with Communist sympathies, which was one of the silly high points of the McCarthy red-hunting era. When the academy designs, by another hand, were finally made public, Wright sniffed that it looked like "a factory for birdmen."

Perhaps there was no real mystery as to why Wright did not get commissions from local, state, or federal governments. Governments are run by committees and administrators responsible to elective officials. They are used to regularity and order, rather than the great flights of fancy that genius produces. Public officials tend to "play it safe" and to avoid controversial figures.

It was not until his later years, when Wright had become almost a national folk symbol of culture, that a handful of governmental agencies lost their timidity enough to employ him.

But old age and white hairs were no guaranty of blanket approval. In 1954 the National Park Service rejected Wright's plan for a restaurant in Yosemite National Park on the ground that it "wouldn't fit into the scenery—it was a mushroom type of thing." [7]

"Politics!" Wright snorted.

In 1956, when Wright himself was eighty-six years old,

the Arizona Technical Board suddenly decided that he must
get an architectural license in that state or quit practicing
architecture there. Two months later the board shame-
facedly granted Wright and several other eminent architects
licenses without examination.

Wright still had some withering blasts for his contemporaries. When he looked at the severely straight lines and
glass façades of the tall apartment buildings that Mies van
der Rohe had built on Chicago's lake front, he called it
"flat-chested architecture!"

Wright, who had made some essays at designing cars,
didn't like the looks of what he saw in the streets. "The automobile is still an old lumber wagon trying to digest four
wheels, and when you see one of these nonsensical creations
with all its chrome and grilles approaching, it looks like a
ferryboat coming down the street and gnashing its teeth," [8] he
said.

But Wright had more satisfactions than disappointments
as an octogenarian. His boyhood city of Madison, Wisconsin, was once more considering a civic center and auditorium. Wright promptly revised his project of fifteen years
earlier for a seven-acre structure at the lake's edge, and a
local committee of enthusiasts began what looked like a
hopeless task of winning public acceptance.

Even the supporters were astonished, however, when the
voters of the city defied the predictions of the experts and
not only approved a bond issue for the auditorium but also
agreed to the lakeside site that Wright had picked and
named him as the architect. This was believed to be the first
time that any large city in the country had voted on a cultural matter like choosing an architect. Although the "com-

mon people" were popularly supposed to have no taste, when they had their first chance to vote on an aesthetic matter, they picked the greatest man available.

Wright's Monona Terrace plan is a "master stroke" because it "extends the heart of a city out over a lake," *Architectural Forum* said in comment on a double-page spread about the project. "Its effect on central Madison will be that of a megaphone—a space megaphone—opening out the tight little existing terminal to the wide drama of Lake Monona. Here is something completely new, something beyond historic emulation, yet its effect will be to enhance the old— not to destroy it." [9]

Nevertheless, the Monona Terrace plan showed the kind of obstacle course that a bold cultural idea must run in this country. Big taxpayers and political opponents of Wright's backers teamed up to get a special law rushed through the Wisconsin legislature, aimed directly against the Monona project, making it impossible. The action became an issue in the next election, and the law was repealed. However, the delays had permitted inflationary costs to enter the picture, and opponents succeeded in tacking on many "additions" to the structure. When it was finally submitted for bids, they were prohibitive.

Wright had been able to stave off death, but that other inevitability, taxes, gave rise to moments of high drama when Wright threatened to leave the state. He had been paying taxes on the farmlands of Taliesin, but he claimed exemption for the Taliesin buildings on the ground that they were part of an architectural school. After all, was not Taliesin approved by the federal government as an architectural school under the GI Bill of Rights?

But the Wisconsin supreme court refused to see it that

way. The court ruled that there wasn't any regular curriculum or set of textbooks and upheld an order against Wright for some $18,000 in back taxes. Wright was in New York when the decision was handed down in November, 1955. Furious, he telephoned newspapers in Madison that he would "unroof" all the buildings at Taliesin and leave them as a monument to the state's lack of appreciation of his work. He threatened that he himself would leave his native state and move to Arizona or New York. Wright even ordered auction sale notices to be printed for the dispersal of the Taliesin herd of pure-bred Guernsey cows.

Friends of Wright rallied to his cause and arranged a testimonial dinner at Madison, at which the governor of the state and many other notables spoke. "He stands not as a pioneer but as a great mountain against homogenized man," said Ralph T. Walker, New York architect and former president of the American Institute of Architects.

Wright, who had never seen the need of any time limit when people called him "the greatest architect of the last 500 years," loved every minute of the profuse tributes. He held up the start of the dinner for nearly an hour so that his students could set up a model of the Monona Terrace project in the center of the dining room. And he stopped some moments in an anteroom, before the march into the head table, to play a few notes on a piano.

"What should I say, overwhelmed as I am by the beauty of this testimonial, the finest I have ever received?" Wright said when he rose to acknowledge the many tributes. "I never would have known the fine esteem of my fellow citizens if it had not been for the adverse court decision."

"It would be ungrateful of me to consider leaving the state now," Wright told newsmen the next day. "The decision of a few officials will not cause me to leave. I was born in Wisconsin and I belong in Wisconsin." [10]

Why not have the state legislature pass a special law declaring Taliesin an architectural school? was the suggestion of George Sellery, former dean of the University of Wisconsin. Everybody thought this was a good idea except the legislators themselves. A few weeks later, when such a bill had been introduced into the legislature, Wright was called to testify before the committee in charge and was treated with indifference and hostility. The bill was killed, but Wright no longer talked of leaving Wisconsin.

The older Wright got, the more elaborate his projects became. The lively touch of the showman was evident throughout his life as he battled to make his architectural ideas prevail over prejudice and ignorance. It came out especially strong in a scheme that provoked instant debate: to build a mile-high skyscraper on Chicago's lake front.

Wright did the original drawing of the ground plan on a piece of paper about the size of a sheet of typewriter paper, grimy with the smudged evidence of frequent erasures as the concept developed. Student helpers promptly transformed it into a giant narrow drawing twenty-two feet high, with the towering mass of the building all done in gold leaf. Clouds even cut across the building at around the 4,500 foot level.

The architect was at his quizzical best when he unveiled the impressive drawing to a group of newsmen in Chicago a couple of days before a testimonial dinner in his behalf, in his eighty-seventh year.

Named the "Mile-High Illinois," Wright said the building would be pressurized like an airplane, have room for parking 20,000 cars, and be served by elevators running a mile a

minute on vertical cog railways, using electricity furnished
by atomic power. The rigid central shaft would be anchored
100 feet into the earth, in the manner of the smaller Johnson
and Price towers, Wright explained. An enraptured woman
reporter who saw the sketch wrote: "a shining shaft, of
golden hue, rose to the sky with a lift that drew the eye
upward. The building looked like a long sword thrust hilt-
first into the earth."

"This 510-story building may be the Eighth Wonder of the
world, but it is as utilitarian as a pair of shoes," Wright told
the reporters. "It is the high city of the future."

"Are you kidding?" was the first question of the reporters.

Wright replied, "I was never more in earnest in my life.
There is nothing in the building that isn't scientific and prac-
tical."

Serious or not, Wright's proposal had the immediate effect
of focusing attention on him once more as a daring and controversial architect—and that may very well have been exactly what he intended. His public explanation was that
somebody had asked him to do a building half a mile high.
"I said 'to hell with that,' and this is what I came out with,"
Wright commented. The architect insisted that he was
merely carrying the skyscraper to its logical conclusion and
that there was no real conflict with the decentralization idea
of Broadacre City.

Some observers thought he was getting revenge for being
left out of the Chicago Century of Progress world's fair
twenty-five years earlier. He had suggested a skyscraper
"half a mile high" for the fair. The Mile-High Illinois would
go in about the same place, and he added that it would
"make the Empire State Building look like a little mouse
next to this building." [11]

Two days later Wright was guest of honor in Chicago at a testimonial dinner attended by over one thousand. Mayor Richard J. Daley had officially proclaimed the day as "Frank Lloyd Wright Day" in Chicago, in honor of the architect. Visibly pleased, Wright must have thought back to the days more than sixty years earlier when he boldly started out to practice architecture—with no encouragement, official or unofficial. He told the dinner crowd that the "Mile-High" was "a 20th century solution to the 19th century impasse created by the skyscraper."

The Chicago dinner was merely a symbol of the avalanche of work and interest centering on Wright. Along with the Mile-High, Wright tossed off a proposal for a "Golden Beacon" fifty-story apartment tower for Chicago's north shore, another taproot building proposal, with a light at the top to be visible all the way across Lake Michigan.

Many of his other dream projects were actually coming true. Just outside Philadelphia, the Congregation Beth Sholem was watching the synagogue that Wright had designed begin to take shape, a shimmering fantasy of translucent glass and bright aluminum, shaped like the ancient Hebrew Ark of the Covenant. A theater project, originally intended for Hartford, Connecticut, but rejected by that municipality, was getting under way in Dallas, Texas. It would set a new high mark in theatrical capability when it opened as the Kalita Humphreys theater. In New York, the Guggenheim Museum had been cleared for construction by municipal authorities.

Even public agencies were beginning to perk up with interest. In California, the Marin County Board of Supervisors voted to ask Wright to submit designs for a new civic center for that "dormitory area" just north of San Francisco's

Golden Gate bridge. The county wanted something that could be done in sections, over a ten- or fifteen-year period, as money became available. The county also asked him to produce a layout for a county fair, and this Wright attacked with great delight because he had always enjoyed county fairs.

The Marin civic center, gracefully spanning a series of low hills, with an anodized golden tint to its exterior matching the color of the high hills around it, did not get into actual construction until just after Wright's death. A small oval-shaped post office, placed near the civic center, was constructed first, and it became the first building Wright designed that was accepted by the federal government. All Wright's tax-supported buildings, in fact, came after his eightieth year.

Another unusual opportunity had presented itself in Baghdad, where King Feisal of Iraq invited Wright to do an opera house, to be financed with oil revenues. Wright flew to Baghdad with William Wesley Peters, his son-in-law and chief assistant. The architect suggested to the king that an island in the Tigris River would make a fine site for the opera house. King Feisal promptly let him have it. Usually architects and public planners have to work years to acquire a central building site, but Wright was getting his with a flip of the royal wrist.

Jubilant, Wright and Peters flew back from Baghdad to start work on the plans, which could run from ten to a hundred million dollars, depending on how extensively the king wanted to venture into culture. Peters kept chortling, "It's in the bag, Dad." But it wasn't. Scarcely had Wright sketched a preliminary layout, employing the ancient ziggurat or wedding cake form of Middle East building, than

King Feisal was assassinated, and the project was shunted aside by the new regime.

There were many other projects. Wright ticked some of them off to a newspaper reporter on the occasion of a violent disagreement with the Madison auditorium committee, which was bickering with him over details of the Civic Center.

He cited Florida Southern College, a twenty-year building project costing some $10,000,000; the $3,500,000 Guggenheim Museum going up in New York; the $1,000,000 Beth Sholem Synagogue in Philadelphia; the $7,000,000 Marin County Civic Center; preliminary plans for a Greek Orthodox church in Milwaukee; a $500,000 theater in Dallas; some forty houses, throughout the United States, some of them for more than $100,000 each, one for a quarter million and one for a half million, and a proposal for a $15,-000,000 Belmont race track grandstand.

"I feel I am wasting my time," Wright had told Madison's auditorium committee earlier in the evening. He pushed back his chair and walked out of the room. "I don't know of a stupider city in the United States. There isn't a good place in it where you can go and get something good to eat and enjoy yourself." Wright had objected particularly to billing the cost of street extensions against funds set aside for the auditorium.

"You're the only client I've ever had who looked a gift horse in the teeth," Wright stormed. "I've built some 769 buildings, but I've never been patronized by a client who wanted me to buy the site for him." [12]

It was past midnight when Wright concluded his talk with the reporter in the hotel room. With his own hand, he wrote out a financial summary of the auditorium, to show that his plans were within the earlier estimates, and went over it line by line with the newsman. In spite of his battle with the committee, he was still going to try to reach an agreement with the members—and eventually did.

The day's events would have worn out any ordinary man, but Wright, though eighty-seven, was living up to his feeling that the time had come to recognize the uncommon man, rather than the common one. He had had conferences in Chicago earlier in the day in an effort to save the Robie house, one of his Prairie Style creations, often called the greatest of his private houses. He had then been driven to Madison, taking nearly five hours, through a heavy snowstorm. In Madison he held an hour's conference with backers of the civic center plan, then spent an hour with Mayor Ivan Nestingen, and then the strenuous, table-pounding session with the auditorium committee, which ended with his walkout.

William Wesley Peters, hovering in the background, said:

"Can I get you a sleeping pill, Mr. Wright? You must be pretty well worn out after a rugged day like this."

"No thanks," Wright replied, almost absent-mindedly. "I want to think about those auditorium revisions. This is the time when I do my best work." [13]

As he had done on so many other nights, "adding tired to tired," Wright moved toward the table, picked up a pencil, and was immediately so absorbed that he seemed not to notice the reporter's departure.

Sixteen

Big Party Man

From his early days in Chicago, when he would break the routine of long days and nights at the drafting board with riotous romps with his children, Wright was especially fond of "dress up" parties. Taliesin's whole history was spangled with big and little celebrations tied to almost any occasion.

Congenial clients were sometimes among the guests, for the Wrights and Taliesin valued people for themselves as much as for their possible help. Sometimes the parties were simply conceived as morale boosters for the apprentice-students, to give them a change from the round of grinding hard work at drafting board or fields.

In the late 1930's, when the Taliesin Fellowship was settling into a pattern of work and play, a Halloween costume party marked the end of the Wisconsin summer of work, just before the whole group took to cars for the drive to winter quarters in Arizona. Apprentices worked in secret to design unusual disguises, to mystify their fellows. Sometimes it would be the clients who were guests. And sometimes the whole Fellowship would be invited to an especially venturesome client's house, to be feted with food and drink. Always there was music, from an ensemble group or the Taliesin chorus, but along with it would go a raucous

skit or a hilarious parody. Wright laughed harder than anyone else at a take-off on the Wisconsin state song, which
began "Taliesin, Taliesin, good old Shining Brow . . ."

The other major celebration of the early years was held at
Easter at Taliesin West and was an elaborate breakfast of
foods that were favorites of Mrs. Wright's. Here the emphasis was on sacred music and formal dress, befitting the occasion, but there were always strings of gas-filled balloons to
bob in the breeze and a coterie of important personages to
be entertained as guests. The Easter celebration marked the
end of the winter's work in Arizona and the beginning of the
trek back to Wisconsin.

A box big enough for a person to hide in would be
trundled into the room each year for Wright's birthday on
June 8, but nobody would be hiding inside. Instead, when
Wright lifted the lid, there was usually some bit of nonsense,
like a scroll hoisted into the air by gas-filled balloons or a
similar surprise. Then, in the bottom of the box, Wright
would take up one by one the special apprentice offerings.
Each person was expected to contribute some original creation to the box. It might be a poem, a drawing of an ar-
rangement for table decorations, a sketch for a house plan—
anything that showed an artistic application by the student
to a problem that interested him. Wright would comment on
each as the blushing student stood nearby.

In the first years of the Fellowship, the birthday parties
were "family affairs," to which no outsiders were invited.
But in the early 1950's the birthday parties began turning
into colorful extravaganzas that took many days of preparation and brought old friends and clients flying in from all
parts of the country. Many were personal friends of the
Wrights, whom they had learned to know during the winters

in Phoenix. Others were municipal or business firm officials
planning or constructing a big Wright project.

A giant bottle of champagne nearly three feet high, un-
corked by Wright himself, led off the festivities at the
eighty-sixth birthday celebration held June 8, 1955, with
sixty-four guests and some sixty apprentices on hand. The
champagne, plus a big birthday cake, had been sent by
plane from New York by a Wright admirer unable to come
himself.

What caught Wright's eye among all the gifts was a pa-
goda-like structure that he soon discovered was a stack of
beautifully fashioned wooden frames. In the center of each
was clear plastic, holding a medal or a scroll awarded to
Wright by distinguished foreign societies. The first one, from
the Imperial Household of Japan, dated from 1919. Some of
the testimonial scrolls had been scorched by the disastrous
fire that swept Taliesin in 1925.

"Why, they're stacked up like cordwood," one spectator
exclaimed as the pile of thirty-eight scrolls and medals from
foreign lands was examined by Wright. Zestful and full of
good spirits, Wright said with a twinkle in his eye as he
looked at the scrolls and medals, "This is one way of brag-
ging."

As to testimonial certificates and medals in general, the
man who had received so many, and from so many parts of
the world, had this to say:

"The only way you know whether they have any value or
not is when you see whom they give the next one to. And
sometimes, then, you feel like giving it back."

Wright kept up a brisk commentary as the documents
were turned over one by one. "That's from Prussia," he said
at one point. "And there's one from the academy in Belgium

to which Franz Hals and the other great ones belonged.
Here are several from Latin America. We have a great many
from there."

"Pure gold," Wright said enthusiastically as he swung
from its ribbon the King George VI medal that he was
awarded in 1940 in England. "They had to wait until after
the war for the actual medal, because they couldn't use gold
then. Just see how heavy it is!"

But it was a much smaller medallion, also of gold, whose
ribbon Wright put gently around his neck and held out for
the guests to see.

"The DeMedici medal," he murmured softly. "It is the one
I prize the most. It is the medal Dante is said to have cov-
eted—and never got." [1]

But the next year's celebration, when Wright was eighty-
seven, topped the previous one as a lavish spectacle. The
architect himself had put in a strenuous day even before the
party began, for he attended ground-breaking ceremonies in
New York for the Guggenheim Museum and then flew to
Wisconsin. Looking and acting anything but eighty-seven,
Wright plunged into the role of active host. He circulated
among the fifty guests, led them up to the hilltop behind
Taliesin for drinks and caviar-spread crackers, and took
some of the notables to his drafting room to show them
sketches of yet unpublicized multi-million-dollar projects.

"Enemies in my house, and they wish me a happy birthday?" he quipped to a reporter and photographer from a
newspaper that had been hostile to him.

To a Madison radio station announcer who telephoned for
a statement, he replied crisply:

"If it isn't worth your while to come out here, it isn't
worth mine to talk to you." [2]

Swinging around to a businessman guest, Wright gestured with his hand to the whole sweep of Taliesin buildings, all of them a tribute to his individual effort, and declared:

"Maybe we are turning now to celebrate the uncommon man. . . . We've had the common man, the fellow who believes just what he sees, and he only sees the things he can put his hands on.

"The common man not only believes that he is as good as every other man, but if the truth were only known, a damn sight better." [3]

Helium-filled balloons carried lighted Japanese lanterns aloft from the Taliesin hilltop as darkness began to move the guests toward the dinner tables. They had scarcely sat down when Mrs. Wright startled them by saying:

"For the first time in the thirty years I have been married to Mr. Wright, I want to propose a toast," she began. "I want you all to drink a toast to the most wonderful person, the greatest architect in the world. And I want to say how glad I am, and how grateful that I have had the wonderful experience of being married to him, and I hope he has many, many more productive years." [4]

Later on, after much music, Wright himself literally stopped the show. The guests were watching a Japanese movie, flown to Taliesin especially for the occasion, but it was no gem. The movie had ground on for some time when Wright, sitting halfway down in the Taliesin theater, said in a loud voice: "Turn on the lights. This has gone on long enough."

No one moved, so Wright got up himself and switched on the lights. "We'll see the rest of this movie some other time," he announced, to the obvious relief of the guests. Then he

invited them all to proceed to the lakeside for more entertainment.

At midnight, at the lake edge, Wright was still full of energy and teased another reporter as they stood beside long
tables furnished with brandy, coffee, and candy. Hundreds
of candles in paper cups floated in bewitching patterns from
the dark farther shore toward the guests. And among the
candles, Taliesin's homemade Spanish galleon, decked with
lights, cruised back and forth, giving out organ music. Two
big bonfires, with great logs burning, warmed the guests,
and the scene was lighted by a semicircle of flaring oil
torches.

"You aren't going to be able to find words to describe
all this, you know," Wright said smilingly to the reporter.

"I think you may be right," the newsman replied glumly.

For his eighty-eighth birthday, the last to be celebrated
before his death, apprentices spent all day roasting lambs
over a spit, the guest list was so long that people could
scarcely move, and the U. S. Information Service, recording
the event for overseas use, filled the dining hall with glaring
lights and miles of electric cable.

In the mid-fifties, Taliesin went through a brief period of
double celebrations each summer. Not only was the Wright
birthday party a heroic affair, but also most of the guests
were invited back in August for another extravaganza, in
which they, rather than Wright, received presents. It was a
wonder that any architectural work at all got done during
the summers. The most magical of these events was a "Four-
teenth Century Italy" production presenting Marco Polo's
return to Venice after his journey to China. The spectacle
began in late afternoon on the borders of the Taliesin lake.

Great posts, from which colored streamers played in the wind, ringed a half circle of chairs and tables near the lake. After the guests were seated, a small ship, the Taliesin galleon with high poop and other likeness to the craft used by Columbus, glided across the water toward the guests, powered less by the brilliantly colored sail than by the electric batteries concealed in the hull.

The boat touched the dock, and a whole company— Marco Polo and his companions—landed, bearing a treasure chest. With elegant gestures the chest was opened, and fine Italian scarves were distributed to all the ladies and gentlemen. Violinists, in exotic costume, made the rounds of the tables, playing special airs at each place. A small drama, involving the Wrights' daughter Iovanna, was enacted on an improvised stage within the half circle of tables.

After these delectations, the fanciful boat cruised up and down the lake, giving off classical music, thanks to a loudspeaker system that neither Columbus nor Marco Polo had envisioned. The guests returned for music to the Taliesin theater, past columns of blazing torches, and then came back to the lake at midnight for a roaring blaze, fireworks, and water-borne candles floating across the lake toward them.

Another year the theme was "Showboat," and the guests gathered near the big drafting room, where a stagecoach had been set up in the parking area, with costumed barkers crying drink and gambling chants. Guests sat at tables in the drafting room for dinner and then laughed at a series of skits and musical numbers, complete with blank pistol shots and the hoarse cries of melodrama.

As he moved past eighty-five, Wright turned more and more to television as his favorite medium, probably because it gave him a chance for the spontaneous quips at which he was so good, and because it brought him into immediate contact with audiences in the millions. He could never resist the blandishments of a New York television personality such as Faye Emerson for a program spot, and in one week, just before his death, managed to appear on no less than eight television shows in New York.

Fifteen years earlier he had been using a hand-crank telephone at Taliesin. Now, in an airplane flying at 20,000 feet, he found it perfectly natural to pick up the plane's phone and give advice from the sky to a New York architectural critic who had troubled him. "This is Frank Lloyd Wright," he boomed over the roar of the engines. "Can you hear me?" The stunned critic, thus mastered from the sky, could only nod his head in agreement.

Twice Wright held public debates with Carl Sandburg, poet and Lincoln biographer who had had many Wisconsin connections. Once they jointly answered a series of questions propounded by *Newsday,* a Long Island newspaper owned by Alicia Guggenheim, wife of a Wright client. On another occasion they swapped less-than-profound remarks over a Chicago television station. In the *Newsday* queries Wright gave his opinions of two contemporary architects, Le Corbusier of France and Mies van der Rohe, a German who was then building aluminum and glass skyscrapers in Chicago.

"I think they are two pretty good men in the wrong place," Wright said. "I think Corbusier should have been a painter. He was a bad one but he should have kept on. No painter can understand architecture. And as for Mies—he is a very honest man and a nice one but he has a heavy scientific list to starboard and he has never gone sufficiently far left. He is in the 19th Century doing the old steel frame that was the great contribution of the 19th Century engineers to building; he is trying to make the old box frame beautiful. He has come as near to it as anybody, but it can't be done." [5]

Wright scored a notable triumph in two television encounters with the formidable Mike Wallace, whose specialty at that time was chewing up celebrities. Wallace would dig up embarrassing or contradictory quotations from the celebrity's earlier writings. He would then give the person the unpleasant alternative of renouncing what he said before or being forced to agree with a currently unpopular stand.

Wright didn't operate that way. Early in the interview he got the upper hand and kept it. The legend popularized later was that during the first interval of the show, when Wallace paused to light a cigarette, Wright quietly leaned forward and made off with Wallace's notes. Whether he did or not, the warm discussion lasted long past the allotted half hour, and it was all recorded. There was enough, after editing out several unorthodox questions of Wallace's, for a sequel performance a couple of weeks later.

In spite of his frequent public appearances, Wright insisted that he was still nervous before every speech—though to the ordinary observer he gave no signs of nervousness and seemed to relish every minute of it. Wright said his nervousness dated back to his country school Friday afternoon speaking practice, which had given him butterflies ever since when he got up to speak.

He was so enamored of television that he even drove in to Madison from Taliesin for a television appearance in his eighty-eighth year over an experimental station with very few listeners. "Well, that wasn't so much of a hanging party as I feared," he said afterward to one of his inquisitors. Another interviewer was Mayor George Forster of Madison, who was becoming an opponent of the Monona Civic Center. Forster remarked during the telecast that his friends had not been impressed when he drove them past one of Wright's houses in Madison. "What kind of friends *do* you have, Mr. Mayor?" Wright shot back at him.

After the grueling half-hour telecast, Wright stepped off briskly into the warm August night, walking down the darkened steps of the studio, disdaining any help from the two persons accompanying him, and even ignoring the handrail. For a man of eighty-eight, this was pretty good. He got into the back seat of the Taliesin car, promptly curled up with a blanket over him, and went to sleep for the forty-mile drive back to Taliesin.

This was one of the secrets of Wright's tremendous energy in his late eighties—the ability to grab a quick nap on the construction site of a church, in the back seat of a car, or just leaning back in a lawn chair in the garden.

"Is it years that determine a man's age?" [6] Wright said defiantly to a reporter, and he was his own best example that they do not. Nevertheless, he knew that even an architectural genius was subject to mortality, so he traveled by plane, to save the moments that were left to him. "Flying effaces travel, and soon ceases to be interesting, but the time saved has become very precious to me," [7] he said.

Seventeen

The Last Easter

Wright himself seemed the gayest and most active among guests and students that Sunday morning in Arizona in 1959, as Taliesin prepared to follow its twenty-five-year traditional Easter festival. The day would mark the rebirth of the season with much music, excellent food, harmonious and beautiful surroundings, and good company. Easter at Taliesin had always meant an occasion for producing a lovely setting in which to hail an ancient festival of creativity.

The architect was already looking forward to a big celebration of his ninetieth birthday in a little over two months at the other Taliesin in Wisconsin. Meanwhile, let the day be filled with music, work, rich laughter, and enjoyment of the human scene. Some one hundred and fifty guests and Taliesin Fellowship members got ready to sit down at one big L-shaped table in the Wrights' patio.

Although it was the end of March, lack of rain had kept the desert flowers and cactus from blooming, so the floor of Paradise Valley was a succession of browns and buffs, interspersed with the brilliant colors of the desert rocks. From the high ground of Taliesin, the guests could look west above the dark green waves of orange groves to the outlines of Camelback Mountain, screening Phoenix. Close at hand were the Taliesin buildings, with their canvas roofs hung under huge red beams. The canvas gave brightness to the interiors without the glare of the sun. Red-tinted floors and walks matched the brilliant desert colors.

Taliesin had put on holiday dress. Dancing strings of helium-filled balloons tugged at their moorings above the patio. As the morning wore on and the desert wind rose, an occasional balloon would be blown against a cactus spine, punctuating the air with a loud pop. Colored beach umbrellas were anchored to the chairs reserved for the more distinguished guests, who also had laid out for them elegant favors of plastic, silk, or metal—toy animals, scarves, dress ornaments, and the like.

Mrs. Wright, under an enormous red straw hat, hurried up and down the sides of the table, making last-minute changes in the place cards to accommodate late arrivals. While she did so, phalanxes of Taliesin youths and maidens advanced on the table with special foods for the Easter fête.

"Look at that hat! And *that* one!" guests whispered to each other as they stood around, waiting for the signal to advance to the table.

Wild Easter hats for the ladies had always been a tradition at Taliesin. There were three-foot picture creations of straw, looking like butterflies as they undulated across the patio, poke bonnets, and high-piled tiers of taffeta, but all with an eye to shade from the sun. The hat that drew the most attention was one that sported a toy rabbit balancing from a trapeze atop the crown, and many a camera was turned to picture it.

The hat topped the head of Mrs. Harold C. Price, Sr., for whose husband Wright had built the majestic Price Tower at Bartlesville, Oklahoma, the eighteen-story central stalk

with apartments branching out from it. He had done a house
for the Prices' son Joe, in Bartlesville, and had recently completed an elaborate winter home for the elder Prices near
Phoenix, all of which had run into plenty of money.

Wright himself soon joined the throng, and spotting Harold Price, resplendent in a bright blue suit, shouted to him
in high glee:

"Harold, how did I happen to leave you enough money to
buy a new suit? I must have overlooked something." [1]

Students who had not been delegated to table service
mingled with the guests, and they also were proper birds of
Paradise Valley. Each student had his own prized items of
festive apparel—a gay-colored waistcoat, a silken cummer-
bund, a gorgeous coat, or a high collar and stock. The
women were even more decorative, with the jewels, hats,
heels, and high hair styling that go with low necks and
sweeping gowns.

Several of the guests were clients like the Prices who had
built one or more houses designed by Wright. Some were
social and business world figures from the Arizona winter
colony. Wright's descendants themselves formed a good-
sized contingent with two sons and a daughter, plus several
grandchildren, including Ann Baxter, stage and television
personality.

"Just one more shot, please, Mr. Wright," several guests
pleaded during a flurry of picture-taking before everyone
moved up to the tables. Wright, in a cream-colored suit and
flat-topped hat to match, and Mrs. Wright with her colorful
straw headpiece, stood with what animation they could muster for a succession of movie and still pictures.

The ceremonies began with music from the long balcony

at one end of the patio. The Taliesin chorus, made up of both men's and women's voices, sang an Easter hymn, "Were You There When They Laid Him in the Tomb?"— unaware that the song would be prophetic.

The breakfast itself, a Taliesin special reserved for Easter, had been served for more than twenty-five years in the desert, and by ten-thirty in the morning the guests were thoroughly ready for it, especially after the warning that there would be no noon meal. The menu included frozen strawberries and a light cake called "baba," eaten with a sweet cheeselike dish named Pascha, made of almonds, egg yolk, and cottage cheese, and filled with raisins. There were also great quantities of colored hard-boiled eggs, plus coffee.

The preparation of the baba is an elaborate annual rite in which husky apprentices, four at a time, plunge their bare arms into the light dough, kneading it vigorously. Four hundred egg yolks are used in the preparation—and the whites appear in later weeks as an infinity of cakes. The babas, baked in cylinder form, are about ten inches in diameter and a little over a foot long. When served, they are cut into inch-thick slices. Guests spread the Pascha cheese on the thick slices and alternated with hard-boiled eggs until they could eat no more.

Children of both guests and students ate at a separate table, and after the breakfast was over, they were furnished with tall baskets for an Easter egg hunt on the grounds near the patio.

"Come on, Mother. Let's go for a walk!" Wright said to his wife as the breakfast festivities finally came to a close. With a general salute to the company with his cane and a smile all around, Wright tucked his wife's hand under his

arm and set off for a tour of the grounds. His back was
straight, his figure trim, and his voice merry as he strode
away for his daily walk.

Wright and his wife returned just in time for one of the
most engaging of Taliesin customs—the "walk-through"
with a departing guest. A visitor who had stayed for a few
days found his packed bags mysteriously spirited from his
quarters as he moved toward the parking area at the other
end of the huge complex of buildings.

Today's visitor—a "middle-sized" executive in a big company—started walking from the cluster of visitors' quarters
on a rise of ground just east of the student family quarters.
As he passed under the great stone and concrete portico
near the dining room, he noticed a few friendly Taliesin apprentices who seemed to be going in the same direction.
More faces appeared as he marched under the great trellis of
red bougainvilleas and came out into the little fountain area
near the movie theater. And as he approached the last
stretch, it looked as if all of Taliesin was marching at his
side, waving, smiling, calling out cheery greetings. By the
time the visitor got to his car, he had sensed the warmth of
the whole Taliesin Fellowship as they waved him into his
car and off down the driveway.

In the early afternoon the religious theme of the day was
emphasized with a film based on the life of Jesus, shown in
the small movie theater that adjoined Wright's private office
and studio. The same desert masonry of great colored rocks
jutting from walls, or embedded in concrete forms, characterized the movie theater. It had a special Taliesin feature:
the low backs of the benches had flat tops so that the audience could eat an evening meal while watching a film.

Taliesin had had a long tradition of Saturday night movies, both in the desert and at the Taliesin near Spring Green, Wisconsin, the summer headquarters of the group. Saturday night was always dress-up night in the theater, with music and a film, usually a foreign import.

During the showing of the religious film on that Easter day, a newspaper photographer who was also a guest tried to get Wright to pose outside with his two sons, Lloyd and David, but Wright's cheerful mood of the morning had vanished, so he merely muttered, "No, no! No more pictures today."

"The camera is a liar. It makes me look old," he told the photographer each time he saw him wandering around, burdened with two cameras around his neck, and carrying a bag of accessories. While Wright said it jokingly, he had an edgy tone in his voice. In the last two or three years Wright had laid down a rule that he would not pose for any more pictures—but each time he would relent in response to some special plea.

What he meant by the camera's being "a liar" was that sometimes it made him look depressingly old. The unmerciful lens would show the long ear lobes and the flabby neck skin characteristic of extreme age. Perhaps also the nervousness of the photographer, confronted by the great man, had something to do with the quality of the picture.

There was time after the film for a nap ("Never start napping after lunch," Wright once warned. "The habit is too hard to break.") and then a light supper. The day ended, naturally, on a musical note. One of the special guests was Miss Carol Robinson of New York, an outstanding pianist. At dusk everyone gathered in the pavilion, a building with a stage, orchestra pit, and high rising bank of seats for two hundred, to hear Miss Robinson on Taliesin's $8,000 Steinway concert grand piano.

Wright sat enchanted, leaning forward at the end of each piece to demand, "More, Carol, more. Don't stop now."

Miss Robinson continued, smilingly game though her arms must have ached, but Wright was insatiable.

"Play some Vivaldi," he urged at one point. "Vivaldi never wrote a trite note."

One more ingenious Taliesin device added color and charm as the day ended. Dozens of lights appeared, outlining the crest of the mountain, which rose a few hundred yards back of the desert buildings. The students had done it with a couple of pails of sand and some brown paper bags. Enough sand was put in the bottom of a bag to hold a candle upright. The sand kept the bag from being blown around by the wind, and the bag shielded the candle. The youths had clambered over the rocky outline of the hill in the early evening, placing the bags and lighting the candles. When darkness came, the outline of the mountain was etched with the delicate glow of the candles.

The device was reminiscent of the similar illumination that concluded parties at Taliesin East, in Wisconsin. Wright loved to finish such parties toward midnight, at the shore of the artificial lake he had created from a stream flowing through the Taliesin grounds. While huge logs burned in a warming bonfire and guests sipped a nightcap drink, the students would set dozens of candles in paper cups afloat on the lake, letting the wind drift them across in changing patterns and streams of soft, glowing color.

The morning after the Easter celebration Wright was up early—probably ahead of most of the guests—for work at the drafting board. He had been creating a design for a new chapel at the Wisconsin Taliesin, to replace the old wood and shingle structure built by the Lloyd-Jones uncles back in 1883. It would contain burial crypts at floor level for himself and his wife, he decided, for even at age eighty-nine, one must begin to think about these things!

He was still concerned, also, with a project he had developed for a new state capitol building for Arizona and hoped he could get a stubborn legislature to see things his way. He had designed a honeycomb canopy roof on stilts, above an area of several acres, to shield a series of buildings and walkways beneath it from the hot Arizona sun.

After years of being scorned and rejected by the government agencies for which he sought to design buildings, he was at last breaking through those barriers of prejudice and blind worship of traditional styles. His design for a big auditorium at Arizona State University at Tempe, just a few miles from Taliesin West, had been well received and would eventually be accepted. Marin County, a favorite home site for San Francisco businessmen, had approved his plans for a vast civic center and county fair layout that would run well over $10,000,000.

Wichita University, in Kansas, was dickering for the design of an education center for its teacher-training program. In Wright's home town of Madison, Wisconsin, his favorite project, the Monona Terrace Auditorium and Civic Center, designed to "marry" the city to one of its surrounding lakes, looked more hopeful.

There seemed no limits, except those of time and energy, to the number of exciting creations that took shape under his pencil at the drafting board. He tired more easily now and was unable to spend more than a few hours each day at the board, but he had many other things to do—lecture offers, more books to write, a constant stream of visitors wanting to discuss new building projects.

Wright took time during the week for a dinner with two newspapermen, where he delighted in sparring with them over how news should be handled. A victim during his middle years of unscrupulous newspaper managements who used his private difficulties for sensational exploitation, Wright could still be mellow toward some newsmen, although he never thoroughly grasped the ideals of objectivity and timeliness.

Though he was often a victim, Wright more than evened the score on other occasions by brilliant use of the press as a sounding board for his own ideas. He was a master of the biting phrase to tear down the false and shoddy in architecture and skillful in presenting his own concepts in poetical clothing that made them seem even more beautiful. All his life he had had the knack of being "good copy" for newspapers, and he knew it.

Yes, life was good in that sunny, warm week in the desert, following the great Easter celebration. Perhaps Wright thought of Louis Sullivan, the "dear master" of his early days who died in poverty and oblivion, his last twenty-five years virtually wasted. And there were so many others—architects, builders, writers—who had flourished in youth and middle age, only to be cast aside, to suffer poverty and even contempt in a bitter and friendless old age. But Wright had broken this pattern, as he had broken so many others. In the fullness of his powers and imaginative creativity, he would soon be back in Wisconsin, to resume the battle over Monona Terrace, to get the Marin County working drawings finished up, to build something new at Taliesin East, and to have a resounding ninetieth birthday celebration with a bigger guest list than ever.

But by the Saturday after Easter, Wright was stricken with an intestinal obstruction and was rushed to a hospital in Phoenix. The doctors decided on an emergency operation despite his age, and two days later the surgery was carried out. He appeared to rally, but then, after two days of intense pain, which drugs could not entirely relieve, he died early on the morning of April 9. The night nurse said that he did not speak at the end but "seemed to give a sigh" and then ceased to breathe. Mrs. Wright and their daughter, Iovanna, who had been constantly at his side, had gone back to Taliesin to get some needed rest and were not with him.

A service of song took place the next day at Taliesin in the desert when Wright's body was brought back to the lovely living room he had created. The students, some of whom had been with Taliesin for twenty years or more, stood to sing the songs that he and they had loved over the years— stood with tears streaming down their faces but managing somehow to sing.

Immediately afterwards the body, in a metal-clad coffin, was placed in a station wagon and driven night and day to Wisconsin. At the wheel for most of the two-thousand-mile drive was William Wesley Peters, Wright's son-in-law through his marriage to Svetlana, Mrs. Wright's daughter by an earlier marriage. It was thus that Wright came back to the ancestral acres, to the Taliesin he had built and then rebuilt twice after disastrous fires, the Taliesin he had lost to banks, regained by his pencil, and enlarged in his green and creative old age.

The funeral, like his life, bore the stamp of his own unconventional pattern. A dozen former students had flown from

New York, Texas, and California to attend the rites. A few
faithful clients were there—and more than a hundred neighbors and friends of the Spring Green area who may have
been skeptics once but had been touched later by his genius
or friendship.

Before the formal service began, Wright's body lay in the
serene living room of Taliesin, scene of visits with clients, the
Sunday night musicals, the entertainment of distinguished
visitors. After the students and others had paid their re-
spects, Olgivanna Lloyd Wright and her daughter Iovanna
filled the coffin with flowers, and Mrs. Wright, the woman
who had brought serenity into the architect's life while she
fortified his spirit for the conflicts in which he was involved,
moved to the small organ in the room and played her own
requiem for the man who had been her life's companion for
more than thirty years.

Then followed a special Taliesin custom. Instead of a
shiny hearse rushing the body to the grave, the casket was
carried down the steps and placed in the box of a plain farm
wagon. The wagon box had been covered with a huge red
velvet drape, and the front decorated with flowers. Two
black horses pulled the wagon, driven by Peters, who was
accompanied on the wagon box by Eugene Masselink, long-
time secretary of Mr. Wright. The mourners fell in behind
the wagon, about forty of them, with Mrs. Wright and Iovanna in the place of honor directly behind the wagon.
News photographers skipped along the road banks at the
sides, getting pictures. As the unusual procession drew
within half a mile of the little chapel, at dusk of that April
day, the chapel bell could be heard tolling.

The same sort of wagon and team had been used for the
funeral of Mamah Borthwick Cheney, forty-five years ear-

lier, and for Svetlana Peters, who had been killed in an auto
accident in 1946. Wright himself had always loved horses
from his farm days, through a succession of riding horses,
beginning with Kano, the big black horse of the Oak Park
period.

"Whoso would be a man must be a nonconformist. . . .
Nothing is at last served but the integrity of your own
mind."

It was the Rev. Max D. Gaebler of the First Unitarian
Society of Madison, of which Wright was a lifelong member,
reading the funeral service. At the graveside Mr. Gaebler, at
the request of the family, read selections from the Book of
Job, Chapter 5, ending, "Thou shalt come to thy grave in a
full age, like as a shock of corn cometh in his season."

And then, as the coffin was lowered into the grave, Secretary Eugene Masselink read the "Work Song" that Wright
himself had composed sixty-three years earlier as his own
statement of independence and integrity.

Later, the students planted over the grave a circle of Wisconsin wildflowers that Wright had loved and set up a narrow triangular building stone from the quarry of Taliesin—
the Taliesin to which he had come in exhilaration or sorrow,
comfort or pain, his home and the home of the Taliesin Fellowship, the young people who sought to learn from him
whose way of life and work were one in boldness, imagination, and daring.

Notes

Source Material for Quotations

CHAPTER 2

1. Morin, Relman. Associated Press article in the *Wisconsin State Journal*, Madison, Wisconsin, June 3, 1956.
2. Wright, Frank Lloyd. *An Autobiography*. New York: Duell, Sloan and Pearce, 1943, p. 9.
3. Wright, Frank Lloyd. *An Autobiography*, p. 18.
4. Wright, Frank Lloyd. *An Autobiography*, p. 21.
5. Wright, Frank Lloyd. *An Autobiography*, p. 17.
6. Wright, Frank Lloyd. *An Autobiography*, p. 23.
7. Wright, Frank Lloyd. *An Autobiography*, p. 46.

CHAPTER 3

1. Wright, Frank Lloyd. *An Autobiography*, p. 50.
2. Wright, Frank Lloyd. *An Autobiography*, pp. 59-60.
3. Wright, Frank Lloyd. *An Autobiography*, p. 104.
4. Wright, Frank Lloyd. *An Autobiography*, p. 87.
5. Wright, Frank Lloyd. *An Autobiography*, p. 101.
6. Wright, Frank Lloyd. *An Autobiography*, p. 102.

CHAPTER 4

1. *San Francisco Chronicle*, October 27, 1963.
2. Morrison, Hugh. *Louis Sullivan, Prophet of Modern Architecture*. New York: W. W. Norton, 1962, p. 184.
3. Wright, Frank Lloyd. *An Autobiography*, p. 126.
4. Haley, Harry, Madison, Wisconsin, building and loan official, conversation with author, 1937.

CHAPTER 5

1. Wright, John Lloyd. *My Father Who Is on Earth*. New York: Putnam, 1946, p. 147.
2. Wright, Frank Lloyd. *An Autobiography*, p. 143.
3. Wright, Frank Lloyd. *The Natural House*. New York: Horizon Press, 1954, p. 51.
4. Wright, Frank Lloyd. *The Natural House*, p. 4.

CHAPTER 6
1. Wright, Frank Lloyd. *An Autobiography,* p. 135.
2. Wright, John Lloyd. *My Father Who Is on Earth,* p. 25.
3. Wright, John Lloyd. *My Father Who Is on Earth,* p. 29.
4. *Rockford* (Illinois) *Star,* May, 1959.

CHAPTER 7
1. Wright conversation with author, 1937.
2. Wright, Frank Lloyd. *An Autobiography,* pp. 175-176.
3. Wright, Frank Lloyd. *An Autobiography,* p. 177.
4. Wright, John Lloyd. *My Father Who Is on Earth,* pp. 71-72.

CHAPTER 8
1. Wright, Frank Lloyd. *An Autobiography,* p. 194.
2. Wright, Frank Lloyd. *An Autobiography,* p. 222.

CHAPTER 9
1. *Drawings of Frank Lloyd Wright.* New York: Horizon Press for the Museum of Modern Art, 1962, introduction by Arthur Drexler, p. 9.

CHAPTER 10
1. Wright, Frank Lloyd. *An Autobiography,* p. 261.

CHAPTER 11
1. Wright, Frank Lloyd. "Broadacre City: A New Community Plan," *Architectural Record,* Vol. 77 (April, 1935), p. 247.
2. This and remaining quotations in this chapter are from conversations between Wright and the author.

CHAPTER 13
1. *Capital Times,* Madison, Wisconsin, June 8, 1938.
2. *Milwaukee* (Wisconsin) *Journal,* April 23, 1938.
3. Wright, Frank Lloyd. *The Future of Architecture.* New

York: Mentor paperback of New American Library, 1963, p. 237.
4. *Capital Times*, October 15, 1941.
5. *Capital Times*, September 24, 1940.
6. *Capital Times*, January 13, 1942.
7. *Capital Times*, January 23, 1942.
8. *Capital Times*, April 1, 1941.

CHAPTER 14

1. Wright, Frank Lloyd. "Forward Concluded," *Architectural Forum*, Vol. 68, No. 1 (January, 1938), p. 101.
2. *Wisconsin State Journal*, June 3, 1956.
3. Copy of telegram in the files of the *Capital Times*.
4. Wright conversation with author.
5. *Capital Times*, October 15, 1948.
6. *New York Times*. "Architect Hits His Field," July 15, 1950, p. 14.
7. *New York Times*, Section VI, Part II, February 1, 1953, p. 64.
8. Herb Caen column, *San Francisco Chronicle*, February 14, 1965.
9. *New York Times*. "Frank Lloyd Wright, Leader of Modern Architectural School, Dies in Phoenix at 89," April 10, 1959, p. 26.
10. From Wright's replies to a series of questions; manuscript in possession of author.

CHAPTER 15

1. *New Yorker*. "Talk of the Town," Vol. XXVIII, No. 21 (July 12, 1952), p. 21.
2. *Capital Times*, October 13, 1955.
3. Kellogg, Cynthia. "First Frank Lloyd Wright House in City to Go on View in Staten Island," *New York Times* (July 3, 1959), p. 20.

4. *Architectural Forum.* "Mortuary for Nicholas P. Daphne of San Francisco," Vol. 88, No. 1 (January, 1948), p. 116.
5. *Architectural Forum,* January, 1948, p. 116.
6. *Capital Times,* November 25, 1948.
7. *New York Times,* December 1, 1954, p. 25.
8. *Capital Times,* October 18, 1956.
9. *Architectural Forum.* "The City," Vol. 106, No. 1 (January, 1957), p. 150.
10. *Capital Times,* February 11, 1955.
11. *Capital Times,* October 16, 1956.
12. *Capital Times,* March 19, 1957.
13. Wright conversation with author.

CHAPTER 16

1. *Capital Times,* June 9, 1955.
2. Wright conversation with author.
3. *Capital Times,* June 9, 1956.
4. *Capital Times,* June 9, 1956.
5. *Capital Times,* June 3, 1956 (reprinted in part from *Newsday,* Garden City, Long Island, New York).
6. *New Yorker,* Vol. XXVIII, No. 21 (July 12, 1952), p. 21.
7. *New Yorker,* Vol. XXVIII, No. 21 (July 12, 1952), p. 21.

CHAPTER 17

1. This and all other quotations in this chapter were made in the presence of the author.

□ Index

Unitarian Church (Madison), 172-175

U.S. Air Force Academy, 182

U.S. Information Service, 197

Unity Temple, 70-72, 74, 101, 166

University of Wisconsin
honorary degree to Wright, 172
Wright studies at, 15, 17, 31

Usonian house, 134-135, 162
See also Low-cost house

Viollet-le-Duc, E. E., 31, 37

Wainwright building, 37, 79

Walker, Ralph T., 185

Wallace, Mike, 200

Waller, Edward C., 46-47

Waller, Edward, Jr., 77, 78

Wasmuth, Ernst, 73-74

Watson, Sir George, lectures, 151

Wendingen, 115

Whitman, Walt, 37

Who's Who in America, 116

Wichita University, 209

Willits, Ward W., 72

Windmill, 64-65

Windows, casement, 58
new fenestration, 58

Wingspread (Johnson house), 126-127, 166

Winslow house, 48-49

Winslow, W. H., 48

Wisconsin Industrial Commission, 13

Wisconsin State Capitol, wing collapse, 14-15

Woollcott, Alexander, 145-148

World's Columbian Exposition, 44

Wright, Anna Lloyd-Jones (Mrs. William Russell Cary Wright), 21, 22, 23, 24, 28, 29, 30, 31, 32, 35, 39, 76

Wright, Catherine, 52

Wright, Catherine Lee Tobin, 38-39, 41, 46, 47, 51, 53, 72, 73, 74, 88, 99, 108, 119

Wright, David, 52, 207

Wright, Frances, 52, 68, 72

Wright, Frank Lloyd
ancestors, 19-20
architectural innovations
Chicago office, 49
Larkin building, 70
Autobiography, An, 119
automobiles
Stoddard-Dayton, 68, 124
Cord, 124
birth, 21
boxing, 39-41
buildings. *See* Beth Sholem Synagogue; Coonley house; Fallingwater; Florida Southern College; Guggenheim Museum; Hillside Home School; Hollyhock House; Imperial Hotel; Johnson Wax Building and laboratory tower; Kalita Humphreys theater; La Miniatura; Larkin build-